The **upside** to
JOB LOSS

Also by Sheila M. Luck:

My Baby's Feet: Choice, Death and the Aftermath

The Challenge of Change: Careers, Callings and Work-Life Crossroads

My Secret Loss: Finding Life After Abortion

Grapple with Guilt, Shed the Shame

Additional books are coming soon. Keep an eye on Sheila's website or her author page on Facebook to hear the latest news.

The **upside** to **JOB LOSS**

Finding Hope for the Future

Sheila M. Luck

Copyright © 2013 – Sheila M. Luck

All rights reserved. No part of this publication may be reproduced, stored in a retrieval system, or transmitted in any form or by any means – electronic, mechanical, photocopy, recording, or any other – except for brief quotations in printed or digital reviews, without the prior written permission of the publisher.

All Scripture quotations, unless otherwise indicated, are taken from THE HOLY BIBLE, NEW INTERNATIONAL VERSION®, NIV® Copyright © 1973, 1978, 1984, 2011 by Biblica, Inc.™ Used by permission. All rights reserved worldwide.

Scripture quotations marked (NIV1984) are taken from the HOLY BIBLE, NEW INTERNATIONAL VERSION®. Copyright © 1973, 1978, 1984 Biblica. Used by permission of Zondervan. All rights reserved.

The "NIV" and "New International Version" trademarks are registered in the United States Patent and Trademark Office by Biblica. Use of either trademark requires the permission of Biblica.

Scripture quotations marked (NLT) are taken from the Holy Bible, New Living Translation, copyright © 1996, 2004, 2007 by Tyndale House Foundation. Used by permission of Tyndale House Publishers, Inc., Carol Stream, Illinois 60188. All rights reserved.

Scripture quotations marked (NKJV) are taken from the New King James Version. Copyright © 1982 by Thomas Nelson, Inc. Used by permission. All rights reserved.

Scripture quotations marked (CEV) are from the Contemporary English Version Copyright © 1991, 1992, 1995 by American Bible Society, Used by Permission.

Scripture quotations marked as (MSG) are taken from The Message. Copyright © 1993, 1994, 1995, 1996, 2000, 2001, 2002. Used by permission of NavPress Publishing Group.

Cover photograph: Copyright 2012, Francisco Tobias, Guatemala City, Guatemala. Used with permission.

Printed and Manufactured in the United States of America

First edition published 2012

Life Sentence Publishing books are available at discounted prices for ministries and other outreach. Find out more by contacting info@lifesentencepublishing.com

Life Sentence Publishing and its logo are trademarks of

Life Sentence Publishing, Inc.
P.O. BOX 652
Abbotsford, WI 54405

www.anekopress.com

Like us on Facebook

ISBN: 978-1-62245-005-3

This book is available from www.anekopress.com,
amazon.com, Barnes & Noble, and your local Christian Bookstore

Dedication

*I dedicate this work to the Lord, our God,
the one who blesses us
with endless opportunities to serve him
and all people in need.*

*My daughters, Chelsy and Krista,
have inspired me to write this book.
They, as young adults, have a lifetime of
God's opportunities ahead of them.*

*I pray that they, you, and I,
recognize and enthusiastically pursue
the opportunities
that God has planned for our lives.*

Contents

Dedication VII

Acknowledgements XI

Introduction XV

Chapter 1: GO BOLDLY! 1

Chapter 2: WHY ME? WHY NOW? 17

Chapter 3: WORRY, WORRY, WORRY 31

Chapter 4: REJECTED AGAIN 45

Chapter 5: YOUR DESTINATION 57

Chapter 6: GOD CALLED 81

Chapter 7: WHEN IN DOUBT, START WITH HIS COMMAND 97

Chapter 8: HERE I AM; I'LL DO IT! 123

Chapter 9: ACTION, ACTION, ACTION 137

Chapter 10: GROWTH OPPORTUNITIES 147

Chapter 11: ONE STEP AT A TIME 161

Appendix A: Using This Book as a Small Group Resource 175

Appendix B: Recommended Reading 195

Memory Verses 199

About the Author 211

Acknowledgements

This workbook would not be possible but for the support and advice provided by several key people.

First, I thank Dr. Thomas J. Wiltzius, PhD, LPC, for his many words of wisdom, starting long before this book was even a thought. I first met and consulted with Dr. Wiltzius when I was employed as a human resources director. He has been a valuable consultant to me in both my business capacity and personally, and he generously continued to provide advice when I chose to write a Bible study entitled, *The Challenge of Change: Careers, Callings and Work-Life Crossroads*. It took only a single meeting with him to help me understand that complete career counseling is a job for experts. I thank God for putting experts into my life.

Additional experts in the career counseling, recruiting, and outplacement fields have graciously donated their time to read this book with an eye toward endorsement. I specifically thank Dan Dieck, Carl Wournos, and John Woerst for their time and encouraging comments.

I have also relied on my friends Kathy King, Sally Swanson, and Thomas Boyle who have read and re-read this manuscript, pointing out points of confusion, dull sections, grammatical errors, and the sections that have left them seeking more information. I greatly appreciate their honesty, thoroughness, and time. I thank God for such supportive friends in my life.

I'd also like to thank my many friends and acquaintances, including those who have participated in my Christian-based workshop, "Work-Life Adventures." They have shared with me their thoughts and stories related to work-life changes. It is through their examples that I have been able to continually build a working understanding of the many types of work-life changes and related challenges.

In particular, I wish to thank Jim Case, owner of Compass Christian Counseling and life coach, Pastor David Lyle of St. Peter's Lutheran Church, Pawleys Island, South Carolina, and Pastor Michael Dismer. Jim Case has extensive work experience in life counseling, career counseling, and employee assistance. His insights regarding life choices and work-life changes added substantially to the quality of *The Challenge of Change*, "Work-Life Adventures," and now this book, an adaptation and compilation of such works. Pastor Lyle shared his personal story about God's call on his life, his thoughts on hearing God's call, and the various ways that God might whisper your name. Pastor Dismer, an insightful and caring Lutheran pastor, has read and endorsed this book.

Of course, no book could be written without the support of my husband and daughters. They so patiently tolerate the numerous books and research papers stacked throughout the house. They listen as I drone on about the new thoughts and ideas I have found, the writings that have inspired me, and the works that have confused me. They have shared their personal insights, humored my requests to take personality profile surveys and tests, and left me alone to pray and write.

My Facebook friends have been very helpful with insightful comments and suggestions for the book cover design. The design selected uses a photograph of our daughter Chelsy while she was in Guatemala. The photo was taken by her friend Francisco Tobias, a talented martial arts instructor and sketch artist. He generously provided permission to use the photo for the cover of this book. I especially like the photo, because I believe it is reflective of the fact that when a person loses his or her job, their world seems to be flipped upside down; but through Christ and a biblical understanding of God's plan for each of us, there is hope, even when our world is upside down. There is hope for a beautiful and exciting future in an upside-down world because we are blessed with this new opportunity to look at ourselves and our work-life futures. With a view from God's perspective, we can identify new directions, discern the path on which God wants us to travel, and go forward with courage. This photo represents hope in an upside-down world.

Lastly, I thank Jeremiah Zeiset and Life Sentence Publishing for encouraging me to modify and reorganize a variety of previous works into this book on job loss, for sharing ideas and suggestions for a solid publishing path, and for enabling me to reach a greater audience during this time of continued high unemployment in our country and around the world.

Introduction

Finding Hope in an Upside-Down World

My initial introduction to this book had some nice comments concerning childhood dreams about careers, and how we might come back to these dreams throughout our lives, especially during times of job loss. As nice as that may be, those of you who have just lost your jobs are likely hurting from the rejection, angry at those who had a hand in your employment termination, and worried about the future. You are looking for help and searching for answers.

Some of you may have received a sixty-day notice that the plant or offices would be closing, as is required by law in many cases. Others may have been escorted out the door alone or with several other co-workers and provided sixty days' pay in lieu of a notice. For a few, the boss said that he wanted to see greater work performance, but it seemed nothing would please him. Some employers may have chosen to re-organize, cut costs, down-size, consolidate operations, merge, or concentrate on core capabilities. The descriptions and reasons used for terminating employment seem endless.

Many understand and can appreciate the company's explanation for the changes. At the same time, most of you believe you were good at your jobs. You worked hard. You were successful. Your work was important and necessary. That's why involuntary unemployment is so hard to accept. It's hard to face the reality that your work-life has changed. It hurts.

Unplanned work-life changes especially hurt because we all take pride in our work. We often enjoy telling people what we do. We like it when people ask about our job. Without a job, we're not sure what to say when asked what we do. Try this answer on for size, "I am looking for new job opportunities in the field of _____. If you have any suggestions, ideas, or leads, I'd love to hear about them." Say it with enthusiasm. Say it without apology. Say it without embarrassment.

Always remember that there is no reason to be embarrassed. There are many people who are unemployed, especially in this economy. Job changes are common; for most people they become opportunities.

According to the Bureau of Labor Statistics, the median number of years that workers had been with their current employer in 2010 was 4.4 years.[1] The number of people who faced some unemployment during 2010 was 25.2 million.[2] People like me, born at the end of the baby-boom years (1957–1964), averaged eleven different jobs by the time they were forty-four years old.[3]

The good news about statistics like these is that employers no longer consider multiple job changes a negative. They see job transitions all the time on résumés and job applications.

This book is for you if you are looking at an unwanted job change and you don't like what you see. I've been in similar shoes. I've had to face unwanted job changes: a pending merger and closure of the offices, a boss with whom I did not see eye to eye, and numerous closed doors. In the face of those struggles, while trying to control the situations on my own, I discovered the truth, the source of my strength, and the foundation for all blessings.

---

1   United States. Department of Labor, Bureau of Labor Statistics. "Employee Tenure, January 2010." *TED: The Editor's Desk*. 27 September 2010. 09 June 2012. http://www.bls.gov/opub/ted/2010/ted20100927.htm

2   United States. Department of Labor, Bureau of Labor Statistics. "Work Experience Summary" *Economic News Release*. 08 December 2011. 09 June 2012. http://www.bls.gov/news.release/work.nr0.htm

3   United States. Department of Labor, Bureau of Labor Statistics. *News Release, USDL-10-1243*. September 10, 2010. 09 June 2012. http://www.bls.gov/news.release/pdf/nlsoy.pdf

Yes, I discovered the upside to job loss, and I want to help you discover the upside as well. I hope that you will find rest in the promises of God, and ultimately know and receive his blessings. I want you to know God's promises, his plans to bless you in your life and work-life with unimaginable blessings, blessings greater than any job that you may have lost or hope to find. God has blessed me in amazing ways and he wants to bless you as well. There is an upside to job loss through God's plan for your life.

So why should you read this book? Will it tell you how to get a job? No. Will this book help you get a job? Yes.

So, you are thinking, *this book will not tell me how to get a job, but it will help me get a job. I don't get it.*

Although this book will not directly teach you how to find new employment, it will help build the foundation necessary for a positive, satisfying, and rewarding work-life change. This book will help to settle the feelings of fear, anger, worry, and rejection. It will help you discover hope for your work-life future, a future built on God's particular plan, a future that involves your total self: your heart, mind, soul, and strength. By understanding the direction that God intends for you and your work-life, you will find it easier to find a new, rewarding employment or work-life situation. Even when uncertain about God's intended path, faith in him will provide all that is needed, and, in time, the upside to your current job loss will become clear.

May the favor of the Lord our God rest upon us; establish the work of our hands for us— yes, establish the work of our hands.
Psalm 90:17

If you know yourself and the direction that God has in mind for you, it will be easier to discern which employment opportunities to pursue. Additionally, it will be easier to clearly and confidently present on your résumé and explain during an interview why you are right for the job. People who take the time to truly understand who they are in God's eyes and to listen to God's call in their lives, exude confidence in their employment searches. Trust God. He has plans for your future, *plans to prosper you and not to harm you, plans to give you hope and a future* (Jeremiah 29:11).

Job loss creates a unique opportunity to evaluate your past, question your present, and dream of your future. According to William Bridges, author of *Managing Transitions*, "stability through change demands clarity about who you are and what you are trying to do."[4] Read that quote again. Let it sink in. *Stability through change demands clarity about who you are and what you are trying to do.* That is what this book is about: finding clarity about who you are and what you are trying to do. This book is about bringing stability to your life, bringing clear direction to your life, and finding God's intended path for your life. When you find God's path for your life, you will discover that there is an upside to job loss, and the upside will often bless you well beyond your imagination. This has been true for me; thus, I know it will be true for you as you seek the Lord and place your trust in him during this time of transition.

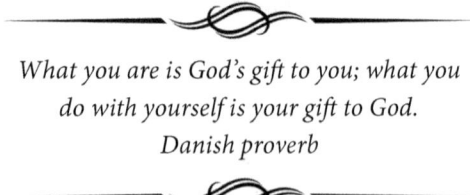

What you are is God's gift to you; what you do with yourself is your gift to God.
Danish proverb

---

4   Bridges, William. *Managing Transitions: Making the Most of Change.* 2nd Ed. Cambridge, MA: Da Capo Press, a member of the Perseus Books Group, 2001 by William Bridges. 107.

If you remain close to God, listen for his voice, and respond to his call on your life and in your work-life, he will open the doors he wants you to enter. If you remain close to God, he will close the doors that he wants you to avoid. If you are not sure about God's call, you can trust that he will provide clarity as he opens and closes doors.

If you remain close to God, he will be with you. What more can you ask for than to have God, the Almighty, Creator of the universe, with you, sitting beside you during an interview? Can you hear the discussion?

"Who's that beside you?"

"My dad."

"Who?"

"My Abba, Father. He's God, the Almighty. He's the boss, the Master of the universe. His pay grade is, like, hey, way higher than yours, and he loves me." Personally, I think it is good to know people in high places, particularly if the one you know is God himself.

The upside to job loss is the opportunity to make our work-life situations better. The upside to job loss is the chance to discover the work-life path that God has planned for each of us.

Through this book, I pray that you will find courage and security by building a personal foundation of strength through Christ. It is with this foundation that you may confront your work-life change, accept your weaknesses, discover how weaknesses may become strengths, and take the next step on the work-life path God intends for you. I pray that you will then identify a positive, everlasting vision for your future, increase your sense of clarity about who you are, tune your ears to the direction God is leading you, and take action, coupled with patience. Then you will discover the next step God has planned for you. Then you will know the upside to job loss.

The rain came down, the streams rose, and the winds blew and beat against that house; yet it did not fall, because it had its foundation on the rock.
Matthew 7:25

CHAPTER 1

GO BOLDLY!

Your word is a lamp for my feet,
a light on my path.
Psalm 119:105

A few summers ago, my husband and I went canoeing on the Crystal River near Waupaca, Wisconsin. We were in a miniature, fiberglass canoe. We were heading over a spot in the river that had a number of rocks, and right after the rocks was a quick turn to the left. Not being canoe-paddling experts, I was quite pleased that we were able to maneuver past the initial set of rocks, even though the path was a bit bumpy. But then came the quick turn to the left, in a spot where the current was too fast, pushing us straight toward the bank. Just before reaching the bank, there was another rock, one I didn't see until it was too late. "Turn! Stop! No, go left, go left, go left!" I shouted to my husband.

"I'm trying!" he shouted back.

Then it happened, slowly but surely, with no physical way to stop the inevitable. The canoe jolted and then lodged on the hidden rock. The river current pushed against the side of the canoe like a bulldozer until it tipped, dumping me into the water. I was drenched. My boat had capsized. There was nothing more to do. Yet somehow my husband fared better than I. He managed to get out of the boat before it went under. He stood there reasonably dry and comfortable.

Although the water was only a couple of feet deep, I had managed to get entirely soaked.

Getting dumped into the cold water as a result of strong currents pushing us into the rocks is a lot like losing a job through no fault of your own. It is also a lot like losing much or most of your savings to a deep dip in the financial markets. For some, it may be a lot like being diagnosed with a life-changing disease. Being dumped into the drink can be a lot like the many bumps in life that hit us. Suddenly, without warning, we find ourselves feeling cold and wet. That warm, comfy feeling of security ceases to exist. Fortunately for me, I was cold and wet for just a day, and the canoe survived as well.

Does any of this sound familiar? Can you relate? How come some people manage to face the capsizing canoe with confidence and peace? From where do they get their strength? What kind of life preserver do they have?

Security is mostly a superstition. It does not exist in nature, nor do the children of men as a whole experience it. Avoiding danger is no safer in the long run than outright exposure. Life is either a daring adventure, or nothing. To keep our faces toward change and behave like free spirits in the presence of fate, is strength undefeatable.
Helen Keller,[5] American author, 1880–1968

A friend relayed a theory to me a few years ago. He said that some of us are pioneers and some of us are settlers. The settlers find a place in the world of life and settle in. They will likely get married. When they purchase a house, they consider all aspects of the deal, expect-

---

5 Keller, Helen. Quote. *Brainy Quote*. 2001 – 2012 BrainyQuote/BookRags Media Network. 12 June 2012. http://www.brainyquote.com/quotes/quotes/h/helen-kelle121787.html

ing it will be their one and only home purchase. They don't intend to move from that house for many years, perhaps not until it is time to go to their heavenly home. Settlers will also find a job, get comfortable with it, and choose to stay in that job for many years. They do not typically relish change.

Pioneers, in contrast, love and seek adventure. They thrive on change. They look to the near future and plan their next move, whether it is a new job, a new town to live in, or simply making new friends. Just when a settler is getting comfortable with the current situation, the pioneer opts to change it.

Especially for settlers, unexpected change so rocks their world that they are often unable to step forward, unable to pick up the pieces and move on. Settlers may get stuck, unable to go on to the next step for years, because they are so hurt by the change or surrounding circumstances.

Allow me to tell you about Henry (real story, fictitious name).

Henry started his working career in the late 1950s or early 1960s, a time when we were taught about and encouraged to work with a sense of loyalty to our employers. At that time, if a person did the job reasonably well, acted with integrity and honesty, and gave the company a little extra time and effort if things were busier than usual, he or she was considered to be a valued and loyal employee. In exchange for the employee's loyalty, the company was loyal to the employee. Only the worst of the worst employees were ever let go. If one's résumé showed more than a couple job changes without a strong explanation, or any job change that was involuntary, this person would have a very difficult time finding new employment.

Henry had grown up in this culture. During his entire working career he was encouraged to believe in the mutual exchange of loyalty between an employer and an employee. Working under the premise of mutual loyalty, Henry thought he would not lose his job, not after twenty-five years with the company. He thought it wasn't possible.

However, the corporate culture of America was changing. Competition was stronger than ever. The financial expectations of a company's shareholders were getting harder and harder to meet. Then the price of oil dropped by two-thirds almost overnight in the mid–1980s, and Henry's employer could no longer be loyal to him, nor to many other employees like Henry. Hundreds of good, loyal employees lost their jobs.

Henry lost his job. He felt the sudden, cold, and wet feeling of unwanted change. His canoe tipped and Henry didn't know how to swim, because he was a settler.

Henry couldn't accept that his employment situation had changed. He was planning to continue working for the same company until he chose to retire at age sixty-five. So, when his job was eliminated, Henry internalized the feelings. He blamed himself for his job loss, a loss that he had no control over. He hurt. He felt shame.

It really wasn't Henry's fault. Henry couldn't control the situation. But Henry believed that he was somehow at fault for his circumstances, for the unemployment boat in which he sat. Henry was devastated. He knew he had done nothing wrong; but even knowing the economics of the situation, Henry viewed his job elimination as a personal slam. Henry slipped into a deep depression, unable to search for work. Sometimes Henry would just sit and watch television all day long. Often, he didn't even want to get out of bed. Henry lost his sense of ambition. He lost his self-esteem. No prodding or encouraging seemed to work. Henry never found another job.

Henry didn't want change to happen. In fact, from Henry's point of view, this change meant failure, and he was devastated by it. Yes, Henry was a settler. The corporate culture in which he initially lived encouraged, praised, and rewarded settlers. During the bulk of Henry's work-life years, pioneers were often viewed as unstable employees, people to avoid.

Sadly, change seems inevitable in today's employment world. The pioneer is rewarded, simply because he is capable of moving and quickly adapting to the new expectations, the new environment, and new responsibilities. The pioneer is agile. Still, we are not all by nature pioneers. Some of us continue to prefer being settlers. Maybe we fear change and tend to proceed reluctantly. Maybe we'd rather stay in a job that is either unfulfilling or even depressing because staying is easier than facing the change. Maybe we have changed jobs but stayed within the same field of work because it felt safe, even though the work was not satisfying.

It is common to dislike change. Some people even fear change, and, as in Henry's case, fear can seriously hamper our ability to move forward.

Yet there are the pioneers. These are people who adjust to change quickly, appearing to adjust with minimal concern. They might say something like, "That's life," and simply take a step forward. Maybe they shake their heads and shrug their shoulders with a look about them that acknowledges moping or complaining would not resolve the situation, and say, "Yeah, well, you know ... stuff just happens sometimes." Other pioneers might say, "I'm sure God has a plan."

For those with certainty about God's plan, faith becomes their life preserver; their strength to change comes from God. Most people understand that life is not fully within their control. They know that life happens, and what happens isn't always good. They know that their canoe might capsize even when they have done everything correctly, but many also know that God is with them.

The insurmountable rocks in our river of life become mere inconveniences when God is with us. I recall and contrast two diverse instances in my life.

The move back to our home state of Wisconsin was going well. We had been in our new location for about six months. Our five and seven-year-old daughters were adjusting to their new environments. Our seven-year-old was learning to speak without her strong Texas accent, so her teacher could understand her better. Our youngest had recovered well from her winter accident on our snowmobile. They no longer worried that our home didn't have an alarm system, finally believing us when we told them that we just didn't need an alarm system anymore, because this small community was much safer than the previous city. We still had some boxes in our basement we hadn't yet unpacked, but all in all we were beginning to make this house our home. We were settling in.

I was also starting to feel settled in my new job, and it seemed like a good job. I liked the people there. They had been very welcoming and accepting of me.

But then change came to my new world most unexpectedly. It was about half past four in the afternoon, time to wind things up for the day and pick up our youngest daughter from the YMCA day care and our oldest daughter from the after-school care program at the elementary school. Rather out of character for him, my boss stopped by each person's desk and invited us to his office for a short meeting. In a quiet tone, he explained that the company was planning to merge with another company. He said that our offices would be closed and all jobs at this location would be eliminated, except for a small number of operational positions. Our specific department would no longer exist. Each of us would be given an opportunity to apply for open positions in the new headquarters location, but in addition to the closure of this office, the merged company expected to reduce the overall head count by at least ten percent. The number of open positions would be very limited. "Any questions?" he asked.

Any questions? I nearly shouted in my mind. *What does he mean by that? How could he hire me away from my good job in Texas just six months ago, tell me that the position was stable, move me and my family across the entire country, and now drop this bomb? Mergers don't happen that fast. He had to have known about the merger before he hired me.* I felt so deceived. I felt like my world was crumbling. I was dropped out of my canoe into the cold water without a life preserver. My life had just been turned upside down.

As I waited for the merger to unfold, many tears were shed. All my stability had been pulled out from under me, like an old, dirty rug. I cried on my sister's shoulder, totally disheartened, feeling rejected as I looked ahead to a very uncertain future.

Fast forward about ten years plus. Life was very different for us by now. We had moved to the other side of the state, my husband transferred with his employer, and I had found a new job. The merger was in the distant past. Even though I desperately looked for new employment at the time of the merger, I ultimately left my most recent position and began a new work-life adventure – writing. Our daughters were doing well. They had good friends and were making good choices for their lives. My husband was in a job he liked. Life was comfortable. Life had become settled.

Life was comfortable, that is, until my faith was again tested. I went to the doctor about a stomach pain. When trying to identify the source of the stomach pain, the doctor discovered a bone with a lesion, a sort of hole. That discovery sent me into a long series of tests to determine whether or not I had a cancer called multiple myeloma. The usual prognosis for this type of cancer is not good, although medical strides have been made. A diagnosis of this type of cancer can be very bad news indeed. My mind ran through all the scenarios. *What about treatments? What if they are not successful? Will they only serve to slow down the progression of the cancer? Do I need to plan for the worst? How does one plan for the worst?* Yet even with these questions, I felt a sense of strength. I knew that I just needed to get through the tests and then deal with the hand I had been dealt.

The tests were negative. I was cancer free.

After the dust settled, I said to my sister, "It's funny about the difference God makes in your life. Remember the days of that merger, when I felt so devastated? I thought my world was coming to an end. But when facing the cancer tests, whereby a positive test quite possibly meant that my world as I knew it was going to change dramatically, I felt a sense of strength. Even though I was potentially facing a death sentence, I knew I would find the strength to manage whatever came my way. Oddly, I felt so much worse when I thought I was losing my job."

My sister replied, "But at the time of the merger, your job was your life."

"That's what I'm trying to say," I responded. "God is my life today, not my job. God changes everything."

God does change everything. He gives us sufficient strength to face any challenge. First, he has promised to be with us and that we should not be afraid because he will help us. In Isaiah 41:10, God said, *So do not fear, for I am with you; do not be dismayed, for I am your God. I will strengthen you and help you; I will uphold you with my righteous right hand.* No matter how difficult the times may be, God promises to protect us. Isaiah 43:2 states, *When you pass through the waters, I will be with you; and when you pass through the rivers, they will not sweep over you. When you walk through the fire, you will not* be burned; the flames will not set you ablaze. God promises that we will not fall into the drink, or even if we do, he will be with us as our life preserver to give us strength.

"Because he loves me," says the LORD, "I will rescue him; I will protect him, for he acknowledges my name. He will call upon me, and I will answer him; I will be with him in trouble, I will deliver him and honor him."
Psalm 91:14-15

Through God, there is peace in good times and in bad times. The apostle Paul said this same thing in his letter to the Philippians in chapter 4, verses 12 and 13: *I know what it is to be in need, and I know what it is to have plenty. I have learned the secret of being content in any and every situation, whether well fed or hungry, whether living in plenty or in want. I can do all this through him who gives me strength.*

But blessed is the one who trusts in the LORD, whose confidence is in him. They will be like a tree planted by the water that sends out its roots by the stream. It does not fear when heat comes; its leaves are always green. It has no worries in a year of drought and never fails to bear fruit.
Jeremiah 17:7-8

God is our life preserver. He gives us the strength we need to face any obstacle that comes our way.

In today's world change is inevitable. Sometimes God wants us to be pioneers. He may ask us to serve him in a new way. He may want us to learn something new. Maybe change is needed to move us closer to God's plan for our lives.

Sometimes change in our work-lives becomes necessary. Often we don't want to make a change because we don't trust the future, the change is contrary to our past teachings, we are afraid to let go of something that seems to provide security, the change doesn't make sense, or it simply doesn't seem fair. In these cases, we may have to step out in faith, trusting in the Lord, taking one step at a time.

In Matthew 14, starting at verse 24, there is the story about the disciples in a boat. They were in trouble, as they were far from the shore and there was a strong wind creating huge waves. It was about three o'clock in the morning. Imagine being on the scene, huddled on the boat in the middle of a dark and windy night. You try to gain a sense of control by searching the black sky for any indication of the extent of the wind, potential rain, and storm. But you are unable to gain an understanding of the extent of the storm or the danger you may be in because the night sky reveals only darkness. The waves toss your boat. Fear builds.

Then you and the other disciples see something on the waters headed toward the boat. It makes no sense. It looks like Jesus, but that wouldn't be possible. Wait. You look again. It looks like Jesus is walking to the boat. He's not swimming. He's walking … on the water, on the top of the water. "What is that?" someone shouts above the crashing roar of the waves. "Is that Jesus, walking on the water?"

It is Jesus. Then Peter calls out to Jesus and says, "Lord, if it's really you, tell me to come to you, walking on the water." Upon Jesus' assurances, Peter steps out of the boat. He keeps his focus on the Lord, and he too walks on the water. Peter is walking on the water. You can't believe your eyes.

Then you notice Peter's head shift a bit as he appears to look around. He looks at the water. He looks at the waves. Just as he nears Jesus,

Peter falls into the water, no longer able to walk on the surface. Jesus grabs him by the hand and they both climb into the boat.

Then the wind stops.

Peter changed his focus. While focused intently on Jesus, Peter walked on the water. While focused on the wind and the waves, Peter's faith in Christ waivered, and he began to sink. Even then, however, even then with wavering faith, Jesus was Peter's life preserver. In the wind, in the storms of life, keep your focus on Jesus. He will pull you through, providing the strength and ability you need.

Jesus is your life preserver in the rough times, in times of unwanted change. It's okay to get out of the boat, even when the waters are rough and overwhelming, even if you don't know how to swim. Simply keep your eyes on Jesus. Trust him to be with you as you navigate the rough waters and move forward. Jesus walks on the waters, and he will enable you to do so as well.

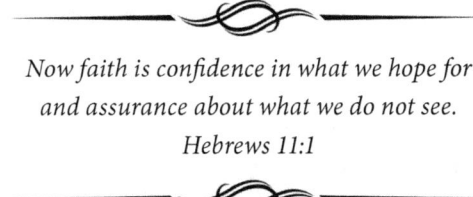

*Now faith is confidence in what we hope for
and assurance about what we do not see.*
Hebrews 11:1

It is so encouraging to me to know that Jesus is my life preserver whenever my circumstances change, or the waters of life are being tossed about by the winds. However, I feel it is necessary to warn you about one small item. If you are a settler, if you don't like change, beware. God often calls for a change in the lives of his people. I know that from personal experience. I also know that from the many examples in the Bible. God moved his faithful ones in so many ways that there is not enough time or space in this book to describe all of the examples of change in the Bible.

Sometimes the change is to teach a lesson, to punish, or to teach us to rely on God alone. For example, Adam and Eve were forced to leave the Garden of Eden due to their disobedience (Genesis 3). The Israelites were required to spend forty years in the desert rather than proceeding on into the Promised Land, when they allowed fear of the inhabitants of the Promised Land rather than faith in God to control their decision about moving forward (Numbers 14).

Sometimes the change is to provide a special blessing. After forty years in the desert, Joshua was able to lead the Israelites into the Promised Land (Joshua 3). Abraham was promised a special blessing when he was called to pack up his entire household and move to a new location, which would become his inheritance. He responded positively in faith, even though he didn't know where he was going at the time of God's call (Genesis 12).

Sometimes the change is for protection. Joseph was told to move his family to Egypt when Jesus was just two years old (Matthew 2:12–14). The move protected Jesus from King Herod's edict to kill all Jewish male children two years old and under.

Some changes are for a special purpose, perhaps to save an entire nation of people. God moved Esther, a young Jewish girl, into the king's harem. She ultimately became queen and was able to save the Jewish people from certain death as a result of the king's edict (see the book of Esther). God also allowed Joseph's brothers to sell Joseph into slavery. Joseph ended up in Egypt and ultimately became the right-hand man in charge of the country during a severe seven-year drought. Joseph was able to save his father's entire family (Genesis 37, beginning at verse 12). Moses moved from his home of wealth and power with the Pharaoh because he could not agree with the persecution of the Israelites as slaves. Moses empathized with the people of Israel, the people of his true heritage. God ultimately used Moses to lead the Israelites out of Egypt (Exodus 2:11–25).

Change is inevitable. Sometimes the change is from God's hand for a particular purpose. Step out in faith and keep your focus on Christ. Allow Jesus to direct your paths and to strengthen you during times of change.

Finally, sometimes it is hard to step forward because the changes feel like swirling floodwaters. In addition to the story about Peter walking on water, do you remember the story about Joshua? Again, try to picture yourself in this scene.

Joshua, your leader, has decided that it is time to cross the Jordan River and head into the Promised Land. You have been living reasonably well in the desert for many years. You have your tent. You have food, manna from heaven. What more could you really want? Yet there has been this talk about the Promised Land, a land flowing with milk and honey. *It sounds real nice, but cross the Jordan River now?* You silently question Joshua's judgment. *Can't he see that the river is at flood stage? We waited this long, so what difference would a month or two make?*

Joshua spoke confidently to the crowds, telling them that God would be with them. He reassured them that God would help them at all stages of this move. He pledged that they would have proof of God's promise to be with them when the priests stepped into the Jordan River. Once they stepped into the river, the river would stop flowing and they would be able to cross the river on dry land.

You think to yourself, *I hope Joshua is right. I pray that God will be with us. But stopping the river from flowing ... will God really do that? I'm glad I'm not one of the priests.*

You watch as the priests take that first step into the rushing waters. You watch with amazement as the waters stop flowing. You praise

God for his faithfulness. You repent for your doubtful heart. (See Joshua 3:9–17 for the actual story about Joshua, God, and the miracle at the Jordan River.)

Did you notice when the river stopped flowing? Did you notice that the priests had to take that first step of faith before the river stopped flowing? Faith sometimes requires us to step forward into the rushing waters before God will step in. Remember, with God all things are possible. If he calls you to do something, to change direction, to make a work-life change, he will be with you. He will be your life preserver and your guide. Keep your faith. Keep your focus on Jesus, and take that first step.

Don't step timidly, filled with fear or doubt. Go boldly. Trust in the Lord.

Have I not commanded you? Be strong and courageous.
Do not be afraid; do not be discouraged, for the Lord
your God will be with you wherever you go.
Joshua 1:9

Reflection & Encouragement

> The truth is that our finest moments are most likely to occur when we are feeling deeply uncomfortable, unhappy, or unfulfilled. For it is only in such moments, propelled by our discomfort, that we are likely to step out of our ruts and start searching for different ways or truer answers. M. Scott Peck,[6]American psychiatrist and author, 1936–2005

---

6 Peck, M. Scott. Quote. *Wisdom Quotes*. 1995-2006 Jone Johnson Lewis. 02 June 2007. http://www.wisdomquotes.com/002576.html

Memory Verse

> *Trust in the LORD with all your heart*
> *and lean not on your own understanding;*
> *in all your ways acknowledge him,*
> *and he will make your paths straight.*
> Proverbs 3:5–6

Closing Prayer

Dear Lord, my heavenly Father, my shepherd and my guide. You lead me through life's changes with a steady hand. Yet, when I face change and paths which seem to lead to the unknown, I forget that you are with me. Forgive me for failing to seek you in times of uncertainty. Help me to see your hand in the changes that I face, and help me to hear your instructions for my first and following steps. Give me courage, Lord, to step forward as you direct my path. I want to go boldly with you. Thank you for your guiding presence. Amen.

Make It Personal

Reading material is only somewhat useful. Applying what you have read brings the material to life. The following questions will help you to apply the main concepts of this chapter to your current work-life situation.

1. Parents, career counselors, and motivational speakers often say, "It's all within your control. Study hard, work hard, pursue your dreams. You can do it."

    a. Is it really within your control? What outside factors can impact your success?

    b. Who is really in control? Who can control everything to the degree that he chooses?

2. Like a house, your ability to withstand the storm depends upon the strength of your foundation. To build a personal foundation of strength, on whom should we build our foundation? Make a list of things you can do to strengthen your foundation in Christ.

3. As M. Scott Peck said, we are propelled by our discomfort to search for better ways. Make a list of the things in your most recent job that you now might like to change for the better.

4. Make a list of the things in your most recent job and other jobs that you really liked and would like to find in your next job.

5. Now try to make a list of the pros and cons of this change from God's point of view. Seek help with this list from strong Christian friends or your church leaders, and through prayer. Compare this list with your answers to questions 3 and 4 above.

6. Pray over these lists, asking God to reveal his will for you concerning this employment change.

CHAPTER 2

WHY ME? WHY NOW?

"In your anger do not sin": Do not let the sun go down while you are still angry, and do not give the devil a foothold.
Ephesians 4:26–27

I couldn't believe they didn't know about the merger when they hired me. I couldn't figure out why they made me a job offer, relocated me and my family, and then announced an intended merger, saying that they were going to close the offices. I moved my family across the entire country just to lose my job. How could they do that? How was I going to find another job in this new city, in this new state, in this place where I had no business contacts, a very limited personal network, almost nothing?

"It'll be okay," my sister would say trying to console me, but to no avail.

It didn't seem okay. I was good at my old job, the one I had before taking this one. It was a great job, one that I loved, one that paid exceptionally well with wonderful benefits, one that offered a strong career outlook. The only problem was that the job did not offer sufficient balance between work and time for our daughters. I was traveling about twenty-five percent of the time. When I was in town, I worked long hours to prepare for the upcoming trips or to compile and analyze the results of the last trip. The job was very demanding and all-consuming. There was very little time for relaxation or family fun. My husband would attend the children's events at the day care and school. He'd ask them to pose, and then take their picture, "so Mommy can see what you did," he'd say. The job wasn't the perfect job as far as family time was concerned, but it was my dream job in all other respects.

Deciding to change jobs was extremely difficult for me. I was looking at giving up my ideal job, my dream career, and the money (one of my primary motivators at the time). I was also looking at moving out of the south, back to the north, back to the cold Wisconsin winters. I always hated Wisconsin winters. I often said that I was a southern girl who was mistakenly born in the north. Giving up all of my career-related dreams was going to be very hard for me to do, even if doing so meant having a better family life; however, the job I had before moving back to Wisconsin simply was not conducive to parenting.

After accepting the new job in Wisconsin, my husband and I spent a lot of time explaining to our young daughters about the importance of moving back to our home state, and why the move would be the best thing for our family. We noted that they would now know their aunts, uncles, and cousins better. We talked about the frequent opportunities they would have to see their grandparents. We explained that the new town was a safer city with less crime. Most of all, we stressed that we would have more time to spend with each other.

We believed that the benefits for our family relationships far outweighed the disadvantages of the jobs: our new jobs were less prestigious, less interesting and less rewarding, with less long-term potential. The new jobs also paid much less than our positions in Texas. We would, however, have more time for our daughters, and we would be closer to our extended families. While that was sufficient justification for making this move, we also had great confidence in our employment-related abilities and knowledge. Thus, we believed it would be just a short time before we would be back on financial and career tracks similar to those we were leaving behind in Texas.

After analyzing all of those factors, the move looked like a good choice. I resigned from my position. My husband was able to transfer.

I was in the new job for only six months when the intended merger was announced. As part of the merger, they planned to close the office in which I was working. I was going to lose my new job. It would be pulled out from under me like an old rug. The new city, having a population of only fifty-five thousand people, had only three similar employment positions, and those were already held by others. Now, instead of having a less prestigious job, with less interesting work, providing lower income, and which was an adjustment that had proven harder to accept than I anticipated, I was going to have no job at all. We were likely going to have to move again.

I had no idea that the work-life changes we chose to make would turn out so badly from a career perspective. I was facing an unwanted, unexpected work-life change with limited to no equivalent employment prospects anywhere in the vicinity.

Our budget was not designed for us to live on only one income. I didn't know how we were going to pay the mortgage, the car loan, and all of the other usual bills with only one of us working.

I knew I'd be welcome to return to my previous employer in Texas, but I couldn't see myself explaining to our daughters that going back to Texas would be the best thing to do without violating my sense of integrity. We had just spent months explaining why moving to our home state was the best thing for our family.

I felt angry. I was angry with my employer for betraying me; I was angry with myself for taking this position, even though I believed that it was the right thing to do for our family at the time; and I was angry with God. I believed when we moved that we were following

God's will for our lives. How could God let this happen to us? We did the right thing. We made the family choice. What more did he want? Did he want me to have nothing, no job at all?

The intended merger took a very long time to evolve because it required numerous governmental approvals. During this time, I went to work each day, doing my job to the best of my ability. However, my attitude suffered. My feelings of betrayal, my anger, and my loss of hope for a future in this job and a career with this employer interfered with my personal happiness and outlook. In time, my self-confidence suffered. I struggled with my expected loss of financial security, fearing for our family's future.

Sometimes when we are angry or fearful, we react in ways that are not really in our best interests.

Allow me to tell you about Mike (true story, different name), who reacted out of fear rather than logic. He didn't resolve his feelings before reacting to the situation. He didn't pause long enough to make logical and wise choices; rather, he made choices based on emotion and panic. Thus, he not only failed to make the best choice, he also made his situation worse.

Mike had been hunting on our family's land. As the day went on, he got turned around, lost in the woods. He frantically searched for something that he recognized, a path out of the woods and back to the house. Finally he spotted the lake and the channel leading from our family's land to the lake. Mike knew there was a path back to the house, if he could get to the other side of the channel.

The channel had filled with weeds and muck over the last forty years due to lack of use. Mike didn't know that he couldn't walk or swim across the channel. It seemed to have more weeds and muck in it than water. However, there was no solid bottom, just seemingly endless muck. In his state of panic, Mike proceeded through the channel without thinking the situation through. As he began to sink, Mike kept going, thinking only about reaching the other side, the side with the path leading back to the house. Suddenly, he found himself neck deep in muck, muck too thick to swim in and too soft to walk upon. It was like quicksand, and Mike was sinking fast. It was a very dangerous situation. He was stuck in the muck, now more fearful than ever. Ultimately and luckily, using his backpack as a flotation device and his gun as a paddle, Mike pushed and paddled his way to the other side – to safety.

If Mike had taken the time to pause and calm down, he would have noticed that he could have simply walked around the channel, if he had merely headed to the east, away from the lake. If he had stopped to look around, he would have seen that the channel ended. If he had taken care of his emotional state first, he would have found a safe route, a solution to his problem.

When I faced the pending merger and expected job loss, I struggled with a feeling of helplessness, being in a situation beyond my control. I struggled with fear over the expected losses: lost job, lost career, lost income, and lost identity (my work had formed my identity at the time). I struggled with a sense of hopelessness and helplessness. I was stuck in the middle of the muck of an unwanted work-life change. I felt that I had no life preserver, no flotation device, no paddle, and no hip waders.

Like Mike, however, if I had just paused to think logically rather than emotionally, I'm sure sensible solutions would have come to me.

Instead, I charged ahead frantically.

I wanted to find new employment immediately, so I would not have to continue working for a boss I thought had been less than truthful, a boss I no longer respected or trusted, a boss I blamed for my changing circumstances. I would not have taken the job if

I had understood the truth about the company's plans. During the interview, I asked my future boss about the stability of the position. He assured me that it was a stable position. Did he lie? What did he know at the time of the interview? I accused him and I blamed him.

I was fearful and angry. I tried to bury the anger inside, trying to wear a face of confidence as I reported to work each day. I tried to hide my rage as I began looking for new employment. I struggled with my anger and my fears, shedding many tears each evening. Like Mike, I reacted when I should have paused and resolved my feelings of anger and fear of loss first.

When the change is not part of our personal plans, our emotions may run rampant. We may face anger, discouragement, disappointment, grief, worry, fear, or a broken heart.

Pause. Stop. Let it rest. Resolve the negative feelings first. Breathe.

As much as we think we can hide our feelings beneath a face of self-confidence, our fears and anger will shine through in a job interview as a lack of self-confidence and disgruntlement. These feelings must be resolved before seeking new employment. I know this from both personal and professional experience. When I worked as a human resources director, I conducted many, many job interviews. It was painfully obvious when a job candidate came to the interview still struggling with anger over their current or recent past employment situation. Their tone, word choice, and body language betrayed their true feelings almost every time.

An angry job candidate will not get hired. The anger and frustration bleeds into the person's work product and attitude, interfering with their ability to do their best. Such feelings can also become contagious, impacting the morale of co-workers. Employers, especially during tough economic times, cannot afford to bring on a new employee who is struggling with anger and related feelings. Employers cannot afford to hire new employees who are not at the top of their game, or who will bring down the morale of the rest of the team.

Get rid of all bitterness, rage and anger, brawling and slander, along with every form of malice. Be kind and compassionate to one another, forgiving each other, just as in Christ God forgave you.
Ephesians 4:31–32

"But I can't help how I feel," you might say. "I don't know how to get over my anger."

Yes, your feelings are real, but they can be resolved.

I expressed my anger to certain friends and family members. Some listened quietly and others advised that it was time to put it all behind me. A strong few recommended that I pursue the now ex-employer in court for making false promises when they hired me.

Take revenge. Make them pay for what they did to you.

Revenge sounded good. However, my goal wasn't focused on making my boss suffer or forcing the company to pay me damages. Instead, I wanted an acknowledgement, an understanding and admission that they had been wrong and that their failure to be truthful caused me significant harm financially, personally, and in my long-term career path. I wanted them to understand that they should have postponed hiring me until the merger dust had settled and the plans were publicly known. Then I could have made an informed decision. I wanted an apology and an offer to help me land on my feet.

And maybe, just maybe, if I am to be honest, I wanted my ex-boss to feel the same hurt and betrayal that I felt. Maybe I did want revenge, maybe just a little.

In his letter to the Romans in chapter 12, beginning at verse 17, the apostle Paul says that we are not to repay evil with evil, and that we are not to seek revenge. He states that we are to let go and let God take care of any punishment, discipline, or other results of his wrath. It is important to trust God to take care of those who have done us wrong. Instead of seeking revenge, the apostle Paul states that we are to combat evil by doing good.

Let God handle it? My blood boils and I'm supposed to let God handle it? Not only that, but I'm supposed to be good to my ex-boss? I don't think so! I want justice! I want this situation corrected. I want all those who wronged me to feel the same pain as I feel. I don't want to repay them with good deeds or actions. I don't want to repay them with kindness. Those were my thoughts at the time. Can you relate?

The most frustrating thing was that my boss acted as though there was no problem. He never apologized. He didn't acknowledge that he lied to me during the interview process. (Maybe he didn't lie; maybe he didn't know about the merger when he interviewed me. I may never really know the truth.) He never bothered to chat with me, to empathize with the difficult situation I was now in, or to offer any form of help through contacts he might have or via a job reference. He offered nothing. He said nothing. My anger continued to boil every day while I was still employed and for several months after my employment ended.

Have you ever noticed that it is so much easier to get over being angry with someone when they sincerely apologize for their wrongdoing? There is a sense of satisfaction knowing that the other person recognizes they hurt you. It is easier to forgive a person who admits their wrongdoing and makes an effort to make retribution. It is easier to forgive a person who is sorry for what they did and for the way things turned out, promising to do whatever is possible to prevent such a situation in the future.

Without the apology, it often seems better to seek justice, as we hope to give the wrongdoer what we believe they deserve.

I sought justice through legal action, a choice that may seem logical for an attorney to make; however, that choice was a mistake. I wish I had followed biblical teachings and left the situation in God's hands. Legal action was an attempt to pursue revenge. It harmed relationships with others at the company. It caused me additional stress and frustration. Legal action stole my time and required me to continue dwelling on the situation months longer than would have been likely if I had just left everything in God's hands.

Legal action did not help me feel better. In fact, as the case progressed, I went months without putting my anger to rest, and additional negative feelings and reactions developed. The unresolved, overextended anger led to hostility toward everyone who I imagined was part of the perceived cover-up, jealousy over how others fared by the end of the merger as compared to myself, embarrassing outbursts of anger, and selfish ambition, as my desire for revenge evolved into a greedy desire for justice. How funny. I felt just as the Bible said I would.

> *When you follow the desires of your sinful nature, the results are very clear ... hostility, quarreling, jealousy, outbursts of anger, selfish ambition, dissension, division, envy ... and other sins like these. Let me tell you again, as I have before, that anyone living that sort of life will not inherit the Kingdom of God (Galatians 5:19–21 NLT).*

I may have thought I was seeking justice, but instead I was looking for revenge. By doing so, my anger was not allowed to subside. Seeking revenge when you are angry will not relieve the anger.

Legal action didn't help me to overcome my anger, but God did. First, I continued to draw closer to God through Bible reading, prayer, and worship. Then I found particular strength, assurances, and relief by reading the psalms. David (once a shepherd boy and ultimately a king) wrote many of the psalms. In them are numerous verses in which he complains to God, vents to God, and asks God to take revenge upon his enemies. Ultimately, David praises God and leaves his anger with God, letting it go. Through the psalms, I came to know that God understands our anger, our hurt feelings, and our fears. Through the psalms, I came to know that it is acceptable to tell God your feelings. Through the psalms, I was reassured that God would take care of the situation in the way he saw fit. Through the psalms, I could praise God and find some relief from my anger, knowing that God cared. Through David's example in the psalms, I learned that it is okay to vent your feelings to God and release some of that anger.

When you are finished venting, the time comes to forgive. Only through forgiveness can we truly part with our anger. *Therefore, as God's chosen people, holy and dearly loved, clothe yourselves with compassion, kindness, humility, gentleness and patience.* <u>Bear with each other and forgive one another if any of you has a grievance against someone. Forgive as the Lord forgave you.</u> *And over all these virtues put on love, which binds them all together in perfect unity"* (Colossians 3:12–14). [Emphasis added.]

In the employment context, the employer typically views the situation from what is in the best interest of the overall business, and then takes action accordingly, placing the impact of the business decisions on the employees as a second or lower priority. Today, it is a rare employer that will keep the impact of their business decisions on their employees as a first priority. If your employer or past employer took extra steps to help you find new opportunities, you are one of the lucky ones; your employer understood just how important our jobs and careers are to our personal and psychological well-being and our families' well-being. Once the business decision is made, jobs are eliminated, and the so-called pink slips are handed out, there is often no apology or statement of remorse. Management may try to break the news gently and provide some encouragement. They will often attempt to explain the business necessity for their actions and hope that you and all other impacted employees will understand. However, they will never say they have done something wrong. Nor will they admit that their business decisions have wronged you or the other employees.

There is no apology in the case of job termination, elimination, or other loss, because the employer has simply made an economic business decision. Most often, they have actually done nothing legally or morally wrong, even though it hurts as you find yourself in a difficult situation, at best.

How do we forgive someone who we believe has done something wrong or hurtful to us, but fails to acknowledge or recognize their wrongdoing or our hurt feelings? How do we forgive someone who not only fails to recognize how they have hurt or harmed us, but continually tries to justify their actions?

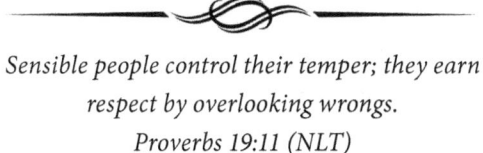

Sensible people control their temper; they earn respect by overlooking wrongs.
Proverbs 19:11 (NLT)

In a straightforward forgiveness model, there are six primary elements of forgiveness. I call them the six Rs of forgiveness: recognition of wrongdoing, repentance, restitution, receiving forgiveness, rendering forgiveness to others, and reconciliation. In the employment context, the employer does not recognize any wrongdoing, so they do not repent or attempt to make restitution (although some will offer a severance package). They don't care if they receive your forgiveness; they don't even seek your forgiveness. Yet to heal your heart, it is important to forgive them if you are harboring anger.

How is that done? I refer you to the words of the Lord's Prayer as used in the New King James translation of the Bible. *And forgive us our debts, As we forgive our debtors* (Matthew 6:12). If you owe someone money, a debt, and they forgive the debt, they simply stop asking for payment. They stop expecting you to pay them. They stop looking to you for the payment. They have forgiven the debt, stricken it from their accounting books, and closed the books forever. They erased it. Going forward, when they turn to their accounting books, they don't see your name. They see no listing of a debt owed by you. Your debt to them is gone. That is forgiveness.

Forgive the company, your past employer, your old boss, and any co-workers you feel may have had a part in your job loss. Review the debt that you believe they owe you and then stop trying to collect on it. Cancel the debt. Erase it from your books. Let it go. Give the debts to God and allow him to be the collection agent, choosing to collect on the debt or choosing to forgive the debt as he wishes. Pray, asking the Lord to provide you with his strength, love, and understanding, so you can let go of the debt with grace and mercy. Pray, asking God to enable you to forgive as he has forgiven you.

Reflection & Encouragement

> Forgiveness is the economy of the heart ... forgiveness saves the expense of anger, the cost of hatred, the waste of spirits.
> Hannah More,[7] English writer, 1745–1833

---

[7] Hannah More. Quote. *Brainy Quote*. BrainyQuote/BookRags Media Network. 2001 – 2012 BrainyQuote. 06 June 2012. http://www.brainyquote.com/quotes/quotes/h/hannahmore129124.html

Memory Verse

Refrain from anger and turn from wrath; do not fret—it leads only to evil. For those who are evil will be destroyed, but those who hope in the LORD will inherit the land.

Psalm 37:8–9

Closing Prayer

My God, my protector and redeemer, your love is without end. Even as I struggle with an unplanned and undesired work-life change, I thank you. I thank you for loving me, for understanding my internal pain, anger, and frustration, and for helping me as I move forward in your love. I don't want to be angry. Give me the strength, courage, and ability I need to overcome this obstacle, emulating your grace by forgiving those who have hurt me. Thank you, Lord Jesus. Amen.

Make It Personal

Reading material is only somewhat useful. Applying what you have read brings the material to life. The following questions will help you to apply the main concepts of this chapter to your current work-life situation.

1. If you are facing job loss, make a list of the things you will miss (your losses) and a list of the positive aspects of the change (your gains). Recognize with respect the losses you are facing. It is healthy to identify them and grieve. Then identify and list what you might do to maintain the positive aspects of this change as you seek new employment opportunities.

2. Make a list of all people with whom you might be angry about your unwanted job change. Include everyone and

anyone, no matter how remote or peripherally involved, as the cause of this situation. Pray over this list of people, forgiving them for the pain they have caused you. (It might be hard to believe, but some on this list may be suffering as they feel they were forced to make such decisions and to publicly support such decisions.) If forgiveness is too hard for you at this time, ask God to allow you to give their debts to him, enabling you to let go.

3. Practical activity can relieve stress and anger and provide other benefits. Do something practical, such as cleaning your closets or garage, exercising, or helping a friend or neighbor in need.

4. Helping others has an amazing way of healing our hearts and resolving our anger. Volunteer with an organization whose mission or work you truly appreciate. Try to find a volunteer opportunity that also uses your particular work-life skills and talents, or will enable you to build your work-life skills and talents.

CHAPTER 3

WORRY, WORRY, WORRY

God is our refuge and strength, an ever-present help in trouble. Therefore we will not fear, though the earth give way and the mountains fall into the heart of the sea.
Psalm 46:1–2

One thing I particularly liked about being twenty-something, and even younger, was that I was invincible. I could do anything I wanted, and it would all turn out okay in the end. I believed I could successfully find a solution for anything, even when I got into a jam. Nothing scared me. Nothing worried me. I believed that I could manage and control everything important in my life.

For example, at that time in life, I loved to race my car along the country roads. I particularly liked taking sharp turns as fast as I dared. A friend had taught me how to lean into the corners at just the right moment, just like a race car driver might do. It was a blast. I loved the excitement of feeling just slightly out of control of the car, but still making the turn. I never thought about what could be in the road on the blind side of the turn. I assumed that I'd be able to react in time to avoid an accident. Insurmountable problems simply didn't exist in my youthful world. Then on one sharp turn along a country road, taking it again too fast for safety, I sped around the corner and there was a cow standing lazily right in the middle of the road. She was big and she looked solid. In an instant I slammed on the brakes with all of my strength, and I held on to the steering wheel ready to swerve as needed. With tires screeching, my car stopped just feet before the cow. She never moved.

Looking back on that incident, I realize now that my 1971 orange Volkswagen Super Beetle, with the trunk in the front and engine in the rear of the car, would not have provided much protection for me if I had hit that cow head-on. With maturity comes a realization that we are not invincible. Sometimes we are not so fortunate and we get hurt.

For seven years I dreamed of going skydiving. My mother told me it was too dangerous. She told me that I could get seriously hurt or even killed. She tried to get me to understand that taking unnecessary risks with my physical safety simply for an afternoon of excitement was not worth it. But I would be fine, or so I thought. Many people go skydiving and never get hurt. I was going to try it.

It was a beautiful day, sunny with a light breeze. It was going to be my second of many intended future jumps. We were about three thousand feet high. I climbed out of the plane and stood on the strut, waiting breathlessly for the jumpmaster to yell, "Jump." He yelled. I jumped, holding my arms and legs out wide in a spread-eagle position. The wind created by the free fall blew my hair back (up, actually) as I waited for the lifting feeling created by the opening parachute. The chute opened as anticipated. It was a beautiful jump, and I was coming down right on target. The view was fabulous, and the world around me was silent. Nothing could be better, until I realized that I was coming down right on top of a parked car, and it was too late to make a directional correction. I lifted my feet to miss the car, but I could not put them down in time to land. I hit the ground with my feet lifted up. I wasn't ready for the impact. The impact was similar to jumping off of a ten-foot-high ledge, with my rump hitting first. I laid there in excruciating pain, unable to roll onto my back, unable to straighten out my twisted body, and unable to get up. I waited in pain for the arrival of the ambulance.

Just as I believed I was physically invincible, until that sky diving accident, I also believed I was invincible in all other aspects of my life. I never doubted that I would find a job upon graduating from college. I believed that I'd just have to apply somewhere and I would get the job. If I was rejected it didn't matter, because I was certain someone else would want me. I had the same feeling when I quit my first job out of college to attend law school. An older friend took me aside and seriously questioned me, nearly chastising me as to why I would risk quitting a good job to go to law school. He couldn't understand why I would make such a decision. I understood it. I wasn't afraid. I didn't worry. I believed in myself. I just knew that I could be successful in all that I did. I was in control of my life.

I got a great job following graduation from law school. I was still invincible. I could still do anything. I continued on my path, always believing that I was in control, and nothing or no one could harm me.

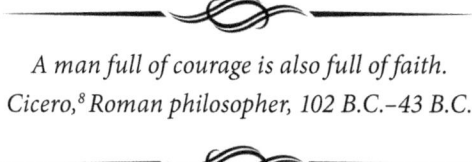

A man full of courage is also full of faith.
Cicero,[8] Roman philosopher, 102 B.C.–43 B.C.

Later, however, after moving back to Wisconsin for family reasons, and after the company merger was announced by the new employer, I discovered that I was not invincible from a career perspective. To make matters more complicated, I was no longer responsible for only myself. We had our daughters to think about. We had a mortgage to pay. We had obligations.

---

8 Cicero. Quote. *To Inspire Quotes.* 1999-2006. 16 March 2007. http://www.toinspire.com/

I was nearly forty years old, and the world that I knew and thought I could control was falling apart, and there was nothing I could do to stop it. I couldn't prevent the inevitable. It was like the sudden landing while skydiving. All was beautiful and running smoothly, until I hit the ground with a thud. It was like the canoe tipping over. I was suddenly underwater without a life preserver.

I was not in control. I could not control everything. I began to worry. Then fear for my future set in. My faith in myself had shattered and anxiety took its place. I worried about money. I worried about damage to my reputation that would result from having lost a job. I worried about how I'd find another job. I began to lose my self-confidence.

Out of fear and worry, even though I was told that finalization of the merger could take as long as two years, I scrambled to adjust our finances, to get a more economical car, and to try to sell our now too-expensive home. I raced to seek new employment, hoping I would find a new opportunity before I was no longer employed. And I struggled with my feelings of grief, anger, rejection, and anxiety.

*Cast your cares on the LORD and he will sustain
you; he will never let the righteous be shaken.
Psalm 55:22*

Worry. I worried, worried, and worried about my future, personally and from a career perspective. I worried, worried, and worried about our family's future, from an economic and security perspective. I worried about paying the bills. I worried about finding new employment. I worried about the potential stigma of having lost my job, even though I had not yet lost my job. I worried about the embarrassment I would feel when I'd have to tell friends and family about losing my job.

I worried about anything and everything that I could imagine that might occur when the company closed our offices.

Let me dissect that sentence. I worried *(I thought endlessly)* about what I would do regarding anything and everything I could imagine *(about imaginary problems)* that might occur *(that had not yet happened)*. Now, allow me to reassemble that sentence. *I thought endlessly about imaginary problems that had not yet happened.* I complained, fretted, and stressed about things that had only been imagined. I stressed over things that were not real, at least not yet.

How valuable was that mental effort and stress? It was absolutely useless. Not one of the problems that I worried about actually occurred. My husband was transferred to another city. I found new employment in the new city. I resigned from the job. Two days after submitting my resignation, the merger was cancelled. I wasted so much energy in worry.

The lesson learned is that it is a waste of time to exercise mental efforts to resolve non-existent problems; it is a waste of time to worry. Worry resolves nothing.

Just like a bad habit, however, it is hard to stop worrying without replacing these unwelcome thoughts with something else.

Finally, brothers and sisters, whatever is true, whatever is noble, whatever is right, whatever is pure, whatever is lovely, whatever is admirable—if anything is excellent or praiseworthy—think about such things.
Philippians 4:8

When I find myself worrying, I've discovered it is helpful to ask if the problem has occurred, if it is imminent, or if I am just imagining a potential but not yet realized problem. If the issue fits in the latter category, I try to live in the present, reminding myself that the issue hasn't manifested itself. Then I pray, giving my worries to Christ. It is important to live in the present and concern yourself with only today's problems, those that have actually manifested themselves. In Jesus' words, *Therefore do not worry about tomorrow, for tomorrow will worry about itself. Each day has enough trouble of its own* (Matthew 6:34).

If something troublesome has happened already, there is nothing to worry about, because you cannot turn back the clock. We only get mulligans in golf. We don't get do-overs, but we can take whatever action is within our control to fix or recover from the situation.

I recall one time when an administrative assistant mistakenly sent a box of private company documents to the wrong recipient. She felt so bad. She began to stress about the trouble she believed she would get into rather than taking action to retrieve the box. When she came to my office to tell me what happened, she was very apologetic, an attitude which I appreciated. However, the apology and the regret and the worry about the ramifications of this mistake did nothing to reduce the potential damage. I told her I appreciated her feelings, but now I would like her to take steps to reduce the damage. Worrying about the results of something that had already happened would not solve anything; but taking steps to reduce the risk of adverse impact would be very helpful. At this point, it was the recovery that mattered, because the mistake had already been made. After some thought and a few phone calls, she was actually able to retrieve the box from the delivery service. It was never delivered to the wrong recipient.

If the problem has not yet occurred, then there is nothing to resolve. If, however, the problem is imminent, maybe there is something that could be done to prepare for the problem, to lessen the blow, to make it easier to recover if it should occur. It is usually wise to be reasonably prepared. It's like taking an umbrella in case it rains. Worrying about the rain will not stop the rain or keep anyone dry, but an umbrella reduces the problem. If we are prepared for anticipated problems, we usually worry less.

In the work-life context, we can prepare for changing circumstances. We can get an umbrella. Most jobs are not totally secure, and sometimes God wants us to make a change. Thus, it is always a good idea to be prepared for change, for the next step, or for a new beginning.

I am a strong believer in keeping my résumé current, even though I'm not looking for employment. I also believe it is good to keep my knowledge up to date and diverse, adding new skills or experiences whenever the opportunity presents itself. Further, I advocate the concept of paying as you go rather than relying on credit. These are just a few of my umbrellas for my work-life.

Perhaps you have ideas that fit your circumstances that would help you or your family prepare for adverse employment changes. Consider what you might do to help your family get through the current changes with a little more ease. Perhaps there are opportunities to adjust your budget, spend less money, increase your savings, or postpone a planned purchase.

One of my work-life endeavors is to provide foreclosure mediation services. In some cases, the homeowners are about to lose their home to foreclosure, yet they continue to drive cars worth more than I have ever paid for a car. They continue their contract for cable television and several other financial expenditures that may not be necessary.

Eliminating unnecessary expenditures is usually an action within one's control. Reducing optional expenses is most often a wise choice, and it will help soften the blow if and when one's job is eliminated.

Other actions that are within one's control include the following: keeping an eye on our employer's financial well-being, investigating similar jobs in the area and working toward building our skills to match such jobs, maintaining relationships with people who work for companies and in jobs that suit one's interests, and volunteering for organizations that have a particular need for one's current skills or desired skills. Volunteering is often a good way to learn or improve our skills in a particular area and to build additional references. With a little thought and conversation, I'm sure that this list of doable items, actions that are within one's control, can easily be expanded.

Are you familiar with the Serenity Prayer? *God grant me the serenity to accept the things I cannot change; courage to change the things I can; and wisdom to know the difference.*[9] Worrying about things we cannot change is no different than worrying about things that are imaginary, things that have not happened and may not ever happen. Worrying about things over which we have no control only tends to add gray hair.

Beyond the doable items, the rest is out of our control. There is, however, still something we can do. The answer lies in our foundation, a firm foundation in Christ.

When we lived in Texas, our first home had no basement. Instead, the house rested on a foundation of concrete, a foundation that was cracked. It was amazing how much the house shifted with the change in ground moisture from morning until evening. We had a sliding glass door leading to the backyard and patio. In the morning, the glass door would be tightly closed at the top of the door, but there

---

9 Source unknown.

was a gap between the door and the door frame at the bottom of the door, exceeding an inch wide. Then, by evening, the entire house had shifted, resulting in a gap at the top of the door, between it and the door frame. The foundation was cracked and the house lacked stability.

Like a house, our stability is only as strong as our foundation. Our foundation is only as strong as its strongest part. Some people build their personal foundations upon themselves, believing that a good education, quality work experiences, and hard work will be all that they need. That was my foundation when my employer announced the intended merger. Upon word of the merger, my foundation cracked. Others build their foundation on wealth, believing that they can overcome any adversity because they are financially stable. In times of recession or depression, wealth can disappear in a heartbeat. The foundation will crack. Many people have been known to build their foundation on their employer, as did Henry (whose story was told in chapter 1). When business needs changed and Henry lost his job, Henry's foundation cracked. Many people build their foundation on their spouse, believing their spouse will care for them. What happens if the spouse dies or there is a divorce? The foundation cracks.

When the foundation cracks, everything relying on it becomes unstable.

As suggested earlier, there are some steps we can take to reduce the severity of the problems that might arise if our foundations crack. However, wouldn't you rather know that your foundation is stable no matter what happens? When the disaster strikes, you can stand firm and stand without worry.

On what could we possibly build our foundations that can withstand all possible disasters? The real question is, on *whom* can we build our foundations so they will not crack?

Jesus promises a firm foundation. Jesus tells us not to worry. *Then Jesus said to his disciples: 'Therefore I tell you, do not worry about your life, what you will eat; or about your body, what you will wear. For life is more than food, and the body more than clothes. Consider the ravens: They do not sow or reap, they have no storeroom or barn; yet God feeds them. And how much more valuable you are than birds! Who of you by worrying can add a single hour to his life? Since you cannot do this very little thing, why do you worry about the rest?'* (Luke 12:22-26).

Let's look closely at those words. Do not worry about your life, your food, your body, or your clothing. Life is more than those things. In God's eyes, the things we tend to worry about are minor items. Jesus even refers to our ability (or inability) to add an hour on to our lives as a *very little thing*. He then questions why we worry about such minor things, pointing out that we are more valuable to God than the birds of the sky, yet God feeds the birds. The answer, then, is that God will feed us too. Instead of worrying about food, clothing, and other things deemed minor in God's eyes, Jesus tells us to seek something far more important. In verse 31, Jesus states that we should seek the kingdom of God. Seek God first and the rest will be provided to us.

Think about that for a moment. Previously I suggested that in times of trouble we should do what is doable, whether in preparation for imminent trouble or as part of the recovery from the trouble. I then referred to the Serenity Prayer, which suggests that we accept the things we cannot change, implying that if you cannot change the situation, there is nothing you can do but accept it. But that is not the full story because, according to Jesus, there is something we *can* do, even in situations we cannot change. We can seek God. Jesus reminds us to first seek the kingdom of God and all other things will be provided to us. This is not just hope. This is a promise.

Seek God.

Do not be afraid, little flock, for your Father has been pleased to give you the kingdom. Sell your possessions and give to the poor. Provide purses for yourselves that will not wear out, a treasure in heaven that will never fail, where no thief comes near and no moth destroys. For where your treasure is, there your heart will be also.
Luke 12:32–34

In Mark chapter 4, beginning at verse 35, there is the story about Jesus and the disciples in a boat during a horrific storm. The waves were breaking over the sides of the boat. The disciples were afraid for their lives. Yet Jesus was calm. In fact, he was so calm during the storm that he slept in the stern of the boat. Finally, the disciples woke him up, fearfully questioning whether he cared about their lives, fearfully seeking his help. With just a few words, Jesus quieted the wind and the waves. Then he admonished the disciples, saying, *Why are you so afraid? Do you still have no faith*? (Mark 4:40).

As we worry about the material things in life that may be adversely impacted by a job loss, things deemed minor from God's point of view, are we doubting God's provision? Are we showing our lack of faith? The disciples were afraid for their very lives as their boat struggled to stay afloat during the storm. Even when their lives were at stake, Jesus questioned the degree of their faith. How much more would he question our faith when we worry during times of job loss? Worry reflects a lack of faith.

Instead of doubting or questioning God in times of trouble, Paul in his letter to the Philippians encourages approaching God differently. He says, *Do not be anxious about anything, but in every situation, by prayer and petition, with thanksgiving, present your requests to God.*

And the peace of God, which transcends all understanding, will guard your hearts and your minds in Christ Jesus (Philippians 4:6–7).

Trust God. Rather than worry, take your concerns to God in prayer and in thanksgiving.

Thank God. Thank him even in times of trouble, in times of job loss, in difficult financial times. Thank him.

"Thank God? I've lost my job, and I'm supposed to thank God for that? What is there to be thankful about?" you might ask. Remember that the apostle Paul encourages us to think about things that are pure, noble, right, true, lovely, and admirable (Philippians 4:8). As you think about such positive things rather than the troubles you are facing, you will know what there is to be thankful about.

Seek God. Praise God. Thank God. Trust God. By doing all these things, we can rest upon a firm foundation. We will have God's peace, as God will be with us. God will provide.

Believing prayer, marked by supplication and thankfulness, that is God's cure for worry.
D. James Kennedy,[10] American pastor, evangelist, and Christian broadcaster, 1930–2007

Reflection & Encouragement

    Fear is living in the past.
    Worry is living in the future.
    To be happy, live in the present.

---

10 Kennedy, D. James. *Turn It to Gold*. Ann Arbor, MI: Servant Publications, 1991 by D. James Kennedy. 77.

Surrender to what you're doing when you are doing it.
Cheryl Gilman, American author[11]

Memory Verse

Cast all your anxiety on him because he cares for you.
1 Peter 5:7

Closing Prayer

Oh, Lord, my heavenly father, I know that you can do all things. You are all powerful. You are the King of kings, God of gods, and Lord of lords. Yet, even though I know these things about you, I often try to manage my life without you. When things do not turn out as hoped, I worry. Forgive me for failing to put my trust in you. Forgive me for having such little faith. As I face unwanted work-life changes, I ask that you take care of all my needs, whether they are physical, economic, emotional, or spiritual. I thank you for your love and grace. Amen.

Make It Personal

Reading material is only somewhat useful. Applying what you have read brings the material to life. The following questions will help you to apply the main concepts of this chapter to your current work-life situation.

1. List the items that might worry you most about a work-life change. Pray over this list, asking God to guide you as you make changes in your life that may reduce such worries.

2. List what is doable by you today or in the near future to help resolve or reduce such worries. Then start doing

---

11 Gilman, Cheryl. *Doing Work You Love*. New York, NY: Barnes & Noble, Inc. by arrangement with The McGraw-Hill Companies, Inc. 1997 by Cheryl Gilman. 75.

the things on your list. Remember to put "Seek God" at the top of your list.

3. List your blessings that will survive any work-life change. Thank God for these blessings.

4. Start an exercise class, walking, bicycling or another regular, physical activity. Physical activity has been proven to reduce stress.

CHAPTER 4

REJECTED AGAIN

> *For I am convinced that neither death nor life, neither angels nor demons, neither the present nor the future, nor any powers, neither height nor depth, nor anything else in all creation, will be able to separate us from the love of God that is in Christ Jesus our Lord.*
> Romans 8:38–39

Rejection. How many times can a person face rejection without losing self-confidence? When I was working as a human resources director, a co-worker told me an anecdote that she had just read. It was apparently written by someone who was tired of the numerous, seemingly endless rejection letters he had received as he looked for work. Most rejection letters say something like this: "Thank you for applying for employment with our company. Although your skills and past work experiences are very strong, we have chosen to give the position to another applicant. We wish you the best of luck in your future endeavors."

Tired of the constant rejection, this person mused about rejecting the next rejection letter. So he wrote something like this:

"Dear Company. Thank you for your careful consideration of my skills and past experiences for potential employment with your company. I have received your rejection letter in response to my application. Although it is well written and clear, I'm afraid I will have to reject your rejection. Your company clearly has a need for someone with my skills and background. Thus, please prepare for my arrival on Monday for my first day on the job. I'm sure you will find my work to be a great benefit for your company."

I wish I could give proper credit to the person who first came up with this idea. I think that it would be great fun to send such a letter. I would love to reject my rejections. There are so many ways to say it:

- I'm sorry, but the rejection you have sent is unacceptable; therefore, I am returning it to you, postage due.

- As I said in the interview, I never accept "no" as the answer, so I'll be there on Monday.

- Please exchange the enclosed rejection letter with an offer letter. I have enclosed a self-addressed, stamped envelope to facilitate this exchange.

- Because I have exceeded all of the minimum application criteria for your school, I assume that the rejection from the college of engineering was sent to me in error. I will plan to start school at the university this fall. Please send information on campus living.

We face rejection not only in response to our job or school applications, but it also hits us in other situations as well. Sometimes we feel rejected as the result of a job loss, regardless of fault. Sometimes the sense of rejection is created internally, when we search for a new work-life opportunity but are unable to identify any possibilities. In all cases, rejection creates a loss: the loss of a dream, loss of a new opportunity, loss of an income, or loss of a job. If our sense of pride or identity is wrapped around or depends upon our work-life, then rejection related to the work-life might also damage our personal sense of self-worth.

I struggled with rejection and the resulting sense of loss when I faced my employer's announced plans to merge with another company and then close our offices.

The merger required extensive governmental approvals, so the actual job changes were not going to occur for several months. Ultimately, the merger was cancelled. However, during the entire period of transition, I looked for other employment, which was not an easy task. We were physically located in an area that had limited employment opportunities for my type of work. In fact, there were no employment openings in the area for my type of work during the ensuing two-year period. The rejection letters came in, not due to my knowledge and experience, but because there were no jobs available. No one was hiring locally, and they did not foresee a need to hire in the near future.

Moving again was the only answer that offered similar employment possibilities for me. However, if I were to find a job that required us to move, then my husband would have to find new employment as well. Thus, moving was not a desirable option from an overall employment standpoint. Furthermore, neither of us wanted to move our daughters again. For the stability of our family life, I wanted to be a settler. Instead, I felt forced to accept a change that only a pioneer could love. Moving meant multiple losses: a loss for me, for my husband regarding his employment, and for our children regarding their home and friends.

I found myself repeatedly questioning why I chose to leave my previous job in Texas. I found myself arguing with God in prayer, questioning why he would allow this to happen, when I had tried to do the right thing by making more time for our daughters. I pleaded with God for new doors to open. I prayed and prayed and prayed. The longer it took to find a comparable position, the worse I felt. My self-esteem plummeted. I had placed most of my personal worth in my job, my career, and my money. The feelings of loss subsided only upon finding new employment.

This same loss of worth and identity reappeared when I left regular paid employment to begin writing, working from my home, and volunteering. Although I believed that this was God's call on my life, it took me a very long time to accept that God really wanted me to stay on this path. So from time to time, I'd apply for regular paid employment when a position opened that interested me. Because I wanted only to do what God intended for my life, with each application, with each interview, I would pray, "God if this is not consistent with your plan for my life, please do not let me get a job offer." Without fail, I got exactly what I asked for: a rejection letter, a rejection email, or a rejection phone call.

God answers prayers, but sometimes the answers are hard on one's ego. While I know that God was telling me to stay the course, keep writing and speaking, keep serving him as I had been doing, the rejections created feelings of failure and a perception that no one wanted me. However, God's path is never a path of failure, even if it includes an occasional rejection. Allow me to emphasize that point: God's path is never a path of failure. He wants our hearts far more than he wants our works.

You need to persevere so that when you have done the
will of God, you will receive what he has promised.
Hebrews 10:36

The story of King Saul and David is a good example of rejection in the workplace. First God rejected King Saul in favor of David. Out of jealousy over David's success and popularity, King Saul tried relentlessly to kill David. (Apparently, when you are the king, you do not need to worry about workplace violence policies.) Yet David did not retaliate.

The story begins at 1 Samuel chapter 16 and continues through to chapter 31.

David, a shepherd, began working for King Saul after David killed a giant named Goliath (1 Samuel 17). In time, because of David's many successes in doing all that King Saul requested of him, David was promoted to a high rank in Saul's army. Everyone was so happy with David that the townspeople began singing songs about David and dancing in the streets, praising his work more than they praised King Saul. As one might guess, this began to anger the king. He became extremely jealous over David's popularity. In fact, he was so jealous that he first tried to kill David by throwing a spear at him. David's successes mounted because the Lord was with him; Saul was not so successful, as the Lord was no longer with Saul (1 Samuel 18:5-15).

David's success continued, and so did Saul's jealousy and his attempts on David's life. Even though King Saul repeatedly tried to have David killed, David continued to serve Saul as best he could, protecting him and comforting him. Ultimately, to save his own life from Saul's hands, David fled into exile.

Intent on killing David, Saul continued to pursue him. But David would do nothing to harm Saul. On one occasion, Saul took three thousand soldiers to find and kill David. David and his men were hiding in the back of a cave. Saul entered the cave to relieve himself, not knowing that David was there. It was the perfect opportunity for David to kill Saul and be free of his relentless pursuit. David, however, believing that King Saul was anointed by God, would not harm him. So he merely snipped off a corner of King Saul's robe. He then told King Saul what he had done, pointing out that he could have killed him but did not do so, hoping to convince King Saul that he would never harm him (1 Samuel 24:10–12).

David left justice to God rather than harming King Saul. David continued to do his job serving King Saul. Only when necessary to save his own life did David leave. Even then, when the opportunity arose, David refused to harm Saul. He allowed Saul to remain in his position of authority.

How is this similar to our work-life situations? Sometimes we might have a co-worker or a boss who doesn't like us or rejects us because we are more knowledgeable or capable than they. Sometimes one worker will go to great lengths to destroy another worker's credibility in order to get ahead or in order to keep their perceived status, fearing that the other worker will be better liked by the boss or by customers or by clients. I had two co-workers like that. One continually tried to take credit for my work. The other believed that my position and experience would get in the way of her rise to the top of the organization. They both worked hard to discredit me in their attempts to further their personal goals.

Although I was angered by their behaviors, I ultimately left each situation in God's hands, trusting him to manage the circumstances as he deemed fit. I moved on to other jobs out of frustration. In hindsight, I believe that moving on to other jobs was the result that God wanted all along.

I often wondered how David could face such extreme persecution from King Saul without retaliating to the fullest extent possible. Throughout his service to Saul and when in exile, David remained close to God in both prayer and praise. David continually turned to the Lord for strength and guidance. I personally found solace in reading the psalms, particularly those written by David. Although all of David's psalms provided to me strength and courage during those times of workplace persecution and thereafter, the following psalm is one of true encouragement.

> *Do not fret because of those who are evil*
> *or be envious of those who do wrong;*
> *for like the grass they will soon wither,*
> *like green plants they will soon die away.*
> *Trust in the LORD and do good;*
> *dwell in the land and enjoy safe pasture.*
> *Take delight in the LORD*
> *and he will give you the desires of your heart.*
> *Commit your way to the LORD;*
> *trust in him and he will do this:*
> *He will make your righteous reward shine like the dawn,*
> *your vindication like the noonday sun.*
> Psalm 37:1–6

We need not fret about those that treat us badly. Instead, if we continue to do good, trust in the Lord, delight in the Lord, and commit our ways to the Lord, God will give us the desires of our hearts. In my case, I didn't know that God had a better plan for my life than what I was seeking at the time. But by allowing God to take charge, I have received more blessings than I ever could have dreamed. The blessings are very different than I had imagined; they are significantly better than my dreams were.

God was with David throughout all of his turmoil with King Saul. In some psalms written by David during his exile, it is clear that David questioned God and cried out to him for help. Although God hears all prayers, his answers are not always obvious to us. However, suffering, persecution, or other adverse events can and should give us new hope. The apostle Paul, in his letter to the Romans, chapter 5, beginning at verse 2, says, *And we boast in the hope of the glory of God. Not only so, but we also glory in our sufferings, because we know that suffering produces perseverance; perseverance, character; and character, hope. And hope does not put us to shame, because God's love has been poured out into our hearts through the Holy Spirit, who has been given to us.* In times of workplace turmoil, in times of job loss, find strength in God's love. With his strength, you will be able to persevere, your character will build, and you will know hope, hope for your future.

How do we find strength in God's love? Often, God uses the people in our lives to share his love and his strength. He often chooses to use the hands and hearts and gifts of people we know. When we approach others for help, we actually bless them with the opportunity to live out God's love. In times of workplace turmoil, remember to seek the help of your family, friends, and acquaintances. Failing to do so deprives others of the opportunity to share God's love with you.

If you are not confident that God is with you through Jesus Christ, or if you have wandered away from him or never have known a personal relationship with him, you may want to take time out to meet with your pastor, priest, or other Christian leaders. If you are not affiliated with a church, begin with a prayer, confessing your sins, accepting Jesus Christ as your Savior, and seeking his love. Through him, you will have all that you need to get through difficult times. Pray:

> *Dear Lord Jesus, I have neither followed your ways nor your commands. Please forgive me for these transgressions, for all of my sins both known and unknown to me. I believe that*

> *you willingly died on the cross for my sins, rose again, and now reign as my Lord and Savior. I accept your gift of salvation, and I am deeply grateful. Thank you for your loving grace, for making me pure in your sight, and for being with me at all times, both in good times and in bad times. Amen. Come Lord Jesus.*

You have just invited Jesus to be the Savior of your life. You now have the opportunity to draw closer and closer to him, in relationship with him. Spend time with him by reading the Bible (I encourage you to start with the gospel of John, which can be found in the New Testament), talking with him through prayer, and honoring him with worship. Talk with others who know Jesus well. Ask them to guide you in your newly discovered relationship. Attend a Christian church, one that continually points to the saving grace of God through Jesus Christ. As you draw closer to Jesus, he will draw closer to you. He will be with you always and you can trust him never to reject you. He will always love you.

Ultimately, the hurts we experience from the rejection of others in the workplace will lose their significance. The sting will fade as it is replaced with the love of God. We each have value, value created by God through his love. Once we know the love of God, we also know our value. As part of God's family, we can move past the rejection and be the person God intended each of us to be.

Reflection & Encouragement

> Nothing is worth more than what someone's willing to pay for it. Even your worth is determined by how much someone would pay. And someone did willingly pay an outlandish price for you. *For even the Son of Man did*

not come to be served, but to serve, and to give His life as a ransom for many (Mark 10:45).

God values you so much that He paid the price of his own son's life for you. You are, as the credit card commercial says, "priceless."

Marsha Mott Jordan,[12] American author

Memory Verse

> *Blessed is the one who perseveres under trial because, having stood the test, that person will receive the crown of life that the Lord has promised to those who love him.*
> James 1:12

Closing Prayer

Dear Father, sometimes things happen to us in our work-lives that make us feel unworthy, unacceptable, or incapable. Our self-esteem may be damaged as a result of rejection. So today I pray, borrowing from the words of the apostle Paul in his letter to the Ephesians, chapter 3, verses 16 to 19: I pray that out of your glorious riches, Lord, that you may strengthen me with power through your Spirit in my inner being, so that Christ may dwell in my heart through faith. And I pray that I, being rooted and established in love, may have power, together with all the Lord's holy people, to grasp how wide and long and high and deep is the love of Christ, and to know this love that surpasses knowledge – that I may be filled to the measure of all the fullness of God. Amen. Come Lord Jesus.

---

12 Jordan, Marsha Mott. *Hugs, Hope and Peanut Butter.* Jacksonville, FL: 2006 by JADA Press. 26. Scripture passage is from the New International Version of the Bible copyright 1973, 1978, 1984 by International Bible Society.

Make It Personal

Reading material is only somewhat useful. Applying what you have read brings the material to life. The following questions will help you to apply the main concepts of this chapter to your current work-life situation.

1. Start a "Wow" box. In it place all thank-you notes and emails, descriptions of personal and work-related accomplishments, and positive quotes from others, whether received in writing or orally.
    a. Add to this box always.
    b. Review the contents of this box when you are preparing for a job interview or performance review.
    c. Review the contents of this box when you are feeling low as a result of rejection.
2. We read in Psalm 37 that we are to delight ourselves in the Lord in times of trouble. Make a list of the things you might do to delight yourself in the Lord.
3. Psalm 37 also states that we should commit our way to the Lord. Write a paragraph which completes the following sentence: In my work-life, I will commit my way to the Lord by _____.
4. Read 1 John 3:1–3. Write a paragraph, stating in your own words and ideas what it means to be a child of God.

Chapter 5

YOUR DESTINATION

For this world is not our permanent home; we are looking forward to a home yet to come.
Hebrews 13:14 (NLT)

I remember when I thought people over twenty-five were old. Now, I don't know when old really starts. Don't get me wrong. I am already noticing the impact of fifty-plus years on my body and my ability to do the things of my younger years. It takes a lot more exercise and much better eating habits to maintain the physical status quo. And the status quo is a far cry from what it once was. Yes, fifty-plus years do have a tendency to show from a physical standpoint.

Today, however, age doesn't seem so obvious to me from an intellectual standpoint. And from a spiritual standpoint, life is just beginning. I am certain that as long as I am still living, God has a plan for me, just as he does for you. In God's eyes, age doesn't matter. Don't forget, he blessed Abraham and Sarah with a baby when they were each nearly one hundred years old.

A common job interview question goes something like this, "Tell me where you see yourself in five years." I remember my younger days, when five years seemed like such a distant projection. *Talk about long-range planning*, I thought. Today, however, my vision for my life goes beyond five years, ten years, or even twenty years. My vision for my life extends beyond death and into eternity. Now I understand long-range planning.

I'll never forget the first time I discovered that a life plan needs to go beyond five years, or even beyond retirement. I was reading the obituaries, being somewhat curious about those whose lives ended earlier than average. On this day, I was reading about a woman who had died. The obituary listed her hobbies. This woman was an "avid QVC shopper." She liked to shop through the television shopping network. This was apparently a point her family thought quite important, but reading that point made me ponder my future obituary.

I then boldly instructed my husband to think of something better to say about me than the fact that I enjoyed shopping. He remained silent, being a man of good judgment, as I tried to give him noteworthy ideas. But even though I was about thirty years old at the time, I discovered that I had not done anything worthy of listing in an obituary. At first it was a disappointing thought. But then I decided I still had time to define my life, make it something of value, something memorable, something obituary-worthy. There was still time.

That was the first time that my vision for life moved beyond the next five years and went all the way to the year of my death, whenever that may be. I just needed to identify something to do that I thought was worth listing in my future obituary. It was an interesting or even laudable goal, but I couldn't think of any ideas.

Several years later, still with no vision other than generally doing something obituary-worthy, I had another epiphany. I was thinking about the death of my first baby, a death I chose through abortion, and a choice that I now know was the wrong choice. I was thinking about forgiveness and reconciliation, about heaven, and about whether my baby was in heaven. I wondered whether my grandmother knew my baby in heaven. Suddenly, a somewhat frightening realization came over me: I discovered that my actions or inactions have eternal consequences.

Vision is far-sighted. It is the willingness to look beyond today and picture what tomorrow should look like. It is what you imagine and hope to be fact at the end of the line, at the ultimate destination. Everyone has imagination to some degree. Everyone can imagine what they think would be a perfect world, the best vacation, a successful career, a successful company, or a quality life. However, it is not necessarily easy to define a vision for our lives and work-lives, even with the best of imaginations.

So we fix our eyes not on what is seen, but on what is unseen, since what is seen is temporary, but what is unseen is eternal.
2 Corinthians 4:18

Why does vision matter?

Lewis Carroll, who wrote *Alice's Adventures in Wonderland* (1865), is quoted as saying, "If you don't know where you are going, any road will get you there." In the book, Alice asks the Cheshire cat which way she should go. He says it depends on where she wants to go. Alice replies that it doesn't matter to her. So he concludes, "Then it doesn't matter which way you go."

Maybe not having a plan works for a weekend drive, but there are other circumstances when knowing where you want to go is critically necessary. Knowing where you want to go, having a vision for the future, helps keep you on the right track. It keeps you focused. Without a vision for your ultimate destination, you will get someplace, but you won't necessarily end up where you want or need to be.

All strong leaders understand the need to have a vision for the future, whether it is a vision for our country, a vision for a company, a vision for a church congregation, a vision for a school, or a vision for the community. In the corporate world, vision helps to bring corporate success. Once the president or chief executive officer identifies the vision, all vice-presidents, directors, managers, and supervisors can set their plans within their functions to pursue the vision. A strong corporate vision enables employees to identify what projects meet the vision, so they can focus their efforts and avoid getting sidetracked with busyness that is not helping the company reach the vision. With everyone understanding the vision, each person can make the best choices within their work assignments.

Vision provides direction in corporate America. It also provides direction in our personal lives and in our work-lives. Within our work-lives, career counselors and school guidance counselors will advise that we look ahead to the desired job at the peak of our career. They essentially ask, "What is your dream for your ideal job? What is the job you want to have by the time you retire?"

Brothers and sisters, I do not consider myself yet to have taken hold of it. But one thing I do: Forgetting what is behind and straining toward what is ahead, I press on toward the goal to win the prize for which God has called me heavenward in Christ Jesus.
Philippians 3:13–14

A well-defined vision considers the ultimate end point, a point at which there is nothing further to consider, nothing more that can be humanly imagined. A well-defined vision is a narrow door, an eternal vision.

Make every effort to enter through the narrow door, because many, I tell you, will try to enter and will not be able to.
Luke 13:24

A Well-Defined Vision Is An Eternal Vision

Career advisors often suggest envisioning the ultimate dream job and working toward that job as a goal. Doing so helps one set a work-life direction. It enables us to know what education is needed, what work-life experiences to pursue, and what people to include in our networks. But what happens when we reach mid-life and the price of oil plummets, causing the company to terminate our positions? What happens when technology changes, and our many years of experience are no longer needed or relevant? What happens when at forty-five years old, the envisioned job is not really attainable? What happens when the work-life vision is broken? On what do we then set our sights?

The author of Ecclesiastes tells us about how easily one can lose sight of the things that truly matter. He writes in chapter 4, verses 7 and 8, *I observed yet another example of something meaningless under the sun. This is the case of a man who is all alone, without a child or a brother, yet who works hard to gain as much wealth as he can. But then he asks himself, "Who am I working for? Why am I giving up so much pleasure now?" It is all so meaningless and depressing* (NLT).

I think the man's question is a critical question. "Who am I working for?"

Colossians 3:23 says, *Whatever you do, work at it with all of your heart, as working for the Lord, not for human masters.* Who are we working for? In all that we do, whatever is our profession, our job, or work-life, we are to do it as though we are working for God.

If we are working for God, then our vision will naturally change. It will change from a personal vision to a vision supportive of God's plan. In the same way as when working for a corporation and the top management has defined the vision for the company, God has defined a vision for this world and a vision for you. In Jeremiah 29:11, God says that he has plans for you, *plans to prosper you and not to harm you, plans to give you hope and a future.* God already has a vision for your life, including a vision for your work-life. When working as though we are working for the Lord, our personal vision changes from things concerning lifestyle at retirement, or a dream job, or money and wealth, or something that might be obituary-worthy, to something else. It changes to what God has planned for his kingdom and for us.

How then does one determine a work-life vision? What is it? How far ahead does one look? Is an eternal vision something that cannot be imagined? Who are we to presume that we can know what God has planned for us? You are right. We cannot know, but God has told us many things about his vision for this world and his plans for us through his Word. And we can start to understand God's plans by letting go of our earthly plans and asking God to lead. Jesus said in Matthew 10:39, *If you cling to your life, you will lose it; but if you give up your life for me, you will find it* (NLT). For true life, on earth and into eternity, seek God's vision, God's plan for your life. Live a life for Christ. Live your life for Christ. Draw close to him and he will guide you, either by communicating with your spirit or by simply opening and closing the various doors as needed.

In Luke, we are told about Mary and Martha, friends of Jesus. When Jesus came to visit them, Martha wanted to be the perfect hostess. She busied herself around the home preparing a meal and doing many other things that she believed were necessary to properly welcome Jesus as her guest. At the same time Mary, Martha's sister, sat at Jesus' feet to listen and hear what he had to say. This frustrated Martha. She thought Mary should be helping her. I can just imagine Martha fuming in the kitchen, wondering when Mary was going to get on her feet and start helping her, so that both of them could relax and enjoy Jesus' visit. Finally, Martha couldn't stand it anymore, and she demanded that Mary help her. In response, Jesus told her that Mary had made the better choice, and that she should not be prevented from listening to him (Luke 10:38–42).

Martha's work was important. Martha cared for Jesus and wanted to do what was right by giving him a proper welcome in her home. But Jesus made it clear that it is even more important to put aside some of our activities, no matter how well-intentioned, so that we can focus on him. Jesus said that Mary was making the better choice. Often, our vision for our work-lives is good, but it can be even better if we focus first on Christ.

God has made everything beautiful in its time. He has also set eternity in the hearts of men (Ecclesiastes 3:11). We were made for eternal life. It is through Jesus Christ that we can have eternal life. It is on Christ that we should focus. By focusing on Jesus, we will find the plan that God has for us.

How does this translate into our daily lives? We've all heard the saying, *You reap what you sow.* This saying comes from the Bible, in the book of Galatians: *Do not be deceived: God cannot be mocked. A man reaps what he sows. Whoever sows to please their flesh, from the flesh will reap destruction; the one who sows to please the Spirit, from the Spirit will reap eternal life* (Galatians 6:7–8). If we work to pursue a vision set on things that please our worldly natures, we will likely face bad news in the end. But if we work to please God, we will reap eternal life. Focus on God and on what pleases God.

Set our hearts on heaven and our minds on heavenly things. Set our vision on Christ. As we focus on Christ, we will want to do things that please the Spirit, things that are true, noble, right, pure, lovely, admirable, excellent, or praiseworthy. From that point, we will begin to identify the work-life vision that God planned just for us. With our hearts and minds fully set on a heavenly vision, our lives will begin to reflect the love of Christ and a life of faith. There is nothing more obituary-worthy, no better vision.

What does a heavenly vision look like? What does an eternal vision look like?

Defining a personal vision, especially an eternal vision, is not an easy task. Entire books are written on the topic of defining one's vision. Corporate executives will often spend days or weeks in retreat to define these things for their companies. Some of us will jump directly to a vision and others of us will need to think about it, considering this chapter and this book a mere introduction to the topic. As an introduction, let's consider some of the likely elements of an eternal vision.

First, it will be focused on something that is important to God. There are many goals that are important to God, all of which can be found by reading the Bible. You can also ask your church leaders to share with you a list of ideals that God considers critical. I can provide a few examples: Jesus prayed for unity between believers, Jesus, and God (John 17:20–26). The greatest commandment is to love God. The second greatest commandment is to love our neighbors (Matthew 22:35–40). The Great Commission is to make disciples of all people (Matthew 28:16–20). Every knee will bow at the name of Jesus (Philippians 2:9–11). We are to honor our parents (Exodus 20:12) and to follow God's commands (Deuteronomy 11:1). Poll your Christian friends, and I'm sure you will get a great number of other examples.

An eternal vision involves something that has an impact beyond oneself. It will necessarily impact others in a positive way. Think about those you remember who are no longer living. Perhaps you can name one or more of our country's heroes. Maybe you recall fondly the wisdom of your grandfather, shared with you as you helped pull weeds from the garden. Maybe, like me, you had a doting aunt who was a wonderful baker. You can still smell her freshly baked cinnamon rolls as she took them out of the oven. Maybe you recall the caring heart of one of your elementary teachers, reflecting on how she went out of her way to ensure that you didn't fall behind when you were ill and missed weeks of school. Maybe you are thinking about your mother, how she took you and your siblings to church each week, and how she prayed that someday each of you would have a lasting love relationship with the Lord. Perhaps, like a friend of mine, you remember the funeral of a favorite uncle. Many, many people attended his funeral, all expressing their appreciation for the small, daily favors that this man did for them. These people have made a lasting impact on the kingdom of God, some on a grander scale than others, and some whose impact may never be fully recognized. Still, their impact was a positive impact, a memorable impact. Their impact had a lasting effect, an effect remembered beyond the grave.

An eternal vision is something that is bigger than us and our known abilities. An eternal vision is something that we likely will not attain without the help of God and of others. When beauty pageant contestants are interviewed, it seems that at least one contestant says she wants world peace. Some of the contestants talk about the importance of solving world hunger, and others talk about stopping child abuse. Each of these objectives is too big for any one person to accomplish alone.

An eternal vision is something we can easily picture. God gave Abraham a vision of being a father of many nations (Genesis 17:3–5). Understanding this vision makes it easier to understand how Abraham was able to trust God to provide when God asked Abraham to sacrifice his son Isaac (Genesis 22:1–14).

Recently, in our home church group discussion, one of the discussion questions encouraged us to describe ourselves as a type of building we would like to be if we could be any type at all. In my heart I immediately knew I wanted to be an amphitheater. Until that moment, I had a vague vision about promoting positive change in this world; but to be an amphitheater for God's kingdom is a vision with clarity. To help others know and live God's love through a written and oral voice, like an amphitheater, is a vision that aligns with something important to God. For each person I reach, there may be a lasting, beyond-the-grave impact. An amphitheater is huge. It's far bigger than me. Anyone can promote positive change, but could my work ever become an amphitheater for God's kingdom? Perhaps yes, but only with God's help. An amphitheater is something I can picture in my mind. It is easy to remember. It's my new vision.

> *Know where you are headed,*
> *and you will stay on solid ground.*
> Proverbs 4:26 (CEV)

I can't define a vision for you. However, I have provided questions at the end of this chapter to help you think about your possible vision. All people are visionary people. Each of us is able to imagine something that is important to us and that could be better than it is today. Forming a perfect work-life vision or personal life vision isn't necessary. In time, your vision will likely evolve. You might face a significant life event that jars your heart, forever changing your vision. Start small. Exercise your imagination by thinking about your vision for a great vacation, your vision for a more beautiful backyard patio, or your vision for a favorite weekend activity. See how that works for you. Then get into the greater vision, one for your personal life and/or for your work-life.

The American Dream: Wealth
Finish high school, get a good education, find a job, and make lots of money. Then you'll be successful. Success equals wealth, which equals happiness. That is the American dream. If you live in America, it is a common vision: happiness through wealth.

Is wealth an eternal vision? What is true wealth?

My father died at age forty; I was nine years old, the youngest of four siblings. After my father's death, my mother faced the difficult challenge of providing for all of us while being limited in work-life and other financial options. As one result, her career-related advice to me often included an admonition to be sure that I could always get a good job that paid well enough to support myself.

I concluded that I needed wealth. I needed success. I needed good pay. I had a vision based on money. At the time I was entering college, it was common knowledge that women, particularly women working in jobs traditionally filled by women (teaching, nursing, administration, or secretarial support), were paid on a lower pay scale. The only way to make substantially more money was to enter a field that was traditionally held by men, such as engineering or chemistry, or by getting an advanced professional degree such as becoming a doctor, dentist, or lawyer.

Well, the choice was easy then, I thought. Pick a major to study in college that women do not typically pick. My vision was all about money, having money enough to support myself and my family, independent of my husband's income, assuming that I would get married someday. So I looked through the college catalogue and discovered a major called industrial technology. The coursework required a number of business courses along with manufacturing-related courses such as sheet metals, cast metals, plastics, woods, power technology, electricity, and more. I noted that I knew nothing about any of these subjects, so it would be a challenge. (I always liked a challenge.) I presumed there were very few women in the field. So I signed up.

I pursued my vision of money, success, and wealth. After college I began working as an engineer for a major corporation. I liked the salary and the people I worked with, but not the job itself. Pursuing the money as my vision did not necessarily make me happy. Three years later, I pursued new dreams and went to law school.

Graduating from law school, I again had a vision of a good job, a successful career, and money. When forming my work-life vision I didn't consider children, our extended family, and other important aspects of my life. My vision for wealth and career success moved my husband and me across the country, away from the people who were most important to us. Our children, the firstborn arriving a couple of years after the move, rarely saw their grandparents; they couldn't name their aunts and uncles; and they hardly knew their cousins. Pursuing a vision based on money did not necessarily take into account the importance of strong relationships in our lives.

When my stepfather died about nine years after we moved to Texas, my mother had gathered a few of his belongings and asked if

I would like to have any of them, particularly since they were gifts we had given to him. Perhaps I had lousy taste in gift giving, because I looked at the things she offered to us and concluded that it was just old, used stuff. The items had no meaning to me, sentimental or otherwise. Money, the basis of my work-life vision, did very little except to purchase items that later became old, used stuff.

I gained success in my job. I was paid well. I felt financially comfortable, even a little spoiled. But my work-life did not accommodate our children and extended family needs or our desires to be near our families. Money bought nothing of real, long-lasting value.

I needed a new vision.

It took me several more years to discover what success is truly about: Success is not about money.

Jesus told a parable about a rich man who had a banner year, a wonderful crop. So he built new barns to hold the new crop, saving all of his wealth for himself. He believed he could build his wealth to such a degree that he could retire from working and simply eat, drink, and be merry. But God called him a fool and told him that he was going to die that evening. So the riches and wealth he had acquired were going to be of no value to him. Jesus concluded the parable by saying, *This is how it will be with whoever stores up things for themselves but is not rich toward God* (Luke 12:15–21).

Do not wear yourself out to get rich; do not trust your own cleverness. Cast but a glance at riches, and they are gone, for they will surely sprout wings and fly off to the sky like an eagle.
Proverbs 23:4–5

Money and the things we buy do not equate to lasting success or wealth. Financial wealth can quickly disappear in tough economic times. Death can quickly turn your life's treasures into old, used stuff destined to be sold for pennies at a yard sale.

The author of Ecclesiastes tells us of the great wealth he had acquired, including herds, flocks, slaves, gold, and silver. But upon reflection, he concluded, *Yet when I surveyed all that my hands had done and what I had toiled to achieve, everything was meaningless, a chasing after the wind; nothing was gained under the sun* (Ecclesiastes 2:11). Jesus tells us to *Watch out! Be on your guard against all kinds of greed; life does not consist in the abundance of possessions* (Luke 12:15). And the apostle Paul said, *But godliness with contentment is great gain* (1 Timothy 6:6).

Defining one's vision requires that we look at many factors, all aspects of ourselves and our lives, and what is important in life from God's perspective. Money is not on God's priority list. It's about relationships – a relationship with God and our relationships with each other.

I grew up near a little town in Wisconsin. We lived on a farm established by my great-grandfather in 1903. He built the farmhouse around 1917. It was a two-story, beige, brick home. As a child I remember thinking that we were the wealthiest people in town. In my heart and mind we certainly had the best house ever built.

It didn't matter that I got only three new dresses at the beginning of the school year as my new wardrobe for school. I never thought we were missing anything when we brought out the box of old swimsuits, summer after summer, and searched for the one that was the closest fit. The joy was in the swimming, not in the swimsuit. I was thrilled when I received a new coat, even if it was a couple sizes too big so that I would be able to wear it for at least two or three winters. Santa

Claus always seemed quite generous, giving us perhaps some new pajamas, a pair of slippers, and other clothes that needed replacing, along with a game, doll, or other toy.

We were a happy family. I thought we were wealthy.

We were happy, but not due to financial wealth. We were happy because of the love within our family, between our friends and neighbors, and within our church community. God had blessed our family in many ways through the people who lived with and around us.

There were also extremely serious times of deep sadness and strife in that farmhouse. My oldest sister died of cancer just five days after her thirteenth birthday. During much of her illness, I had an unexplained blood problem, an extremely low platelet count. Although my health was restored, my parents ultimately faced heartbreak with the death of my sister. Then just six years later, my father died when a blood clot moved into his heart. Our lives as we knew them were shattered.

It was during the times of family pain and sorrow that the value of our extended families and many friends in the community was truly understood and appreciated. It was during these times that the strength and comfort of our Lord was desperately needed, and he never let us down. He was with us along each painful step.

I know now that my childhood home, the farmhouse, wasn't the best house in town. I know now that we weren't financially well off. Yet, we were wealthy. Our wealth was in our relationships with each other and, in particular, in our relationship with the Lord.

Mission

In addition to a vision statement, it is common for corporations to have a mission statement, which briefly describes the field in which the company is going to work to pursue their vision. The vision is the end place, the *where*, the destination. The mission is the *how*. The mission makes the vision personal, whether personal to a department, to a team, or to a particular employee. A thousand people can pursue the same vision, but they might pursue it in a thousand ways, within their niche of expertise and ability, within their realm of influence, and within their realm of authority. Mission is what you do in your life story to reach your vision; it is your *how*.

Let's pretend that we are going on a vacation together. We agree to meet each other in Indianapolis, Indiana, because it is centrally located between our homes. Let's pretend that I live in California and you live in Maine. We have different passions when it comes to vacations. I find the end destination to be the most important part. You find the travelling to be the most important part. You love buses, trains, and automobiles. I go for speed. What time is our flight? We have different schedules. I can spare only a weekend. You have three weeks to spend, most of which will be spent moseying along country roads experiencing true Americana. Do you see the difference? We have the same vision, the same destination: Indianapolis for a weekend. I'm going to fly there. That is my *how*, my mission. You are going to drive the country roads. That is your *how*, your mission.

Discerning your mission can be difficult. However, my friend Jim Case shared a bit of wisdom with me. He said, "No one will find their calling apart from submitting to loving the discipline of God in their own story." God made each of us different, each for a different purpose; and he has placed each of us in our families, communities, and work environments, so that we may live for him within the realm of our own story, in our own lives.

When I first started trying to define my mission, I looked at all of the jobs that I had over the years: babysitting, A&W carhop, waitressing at a local diner, encoding checks at a bank, engineering, legal counsel, teaching, and more. I asked myself, *What did I like most about each job? Why did some jobs feel like pure torture?* Asking those questions helped me to understand what my mission might include. Do I prefer to hop on the airplane or mosey down country roads?

I looked at my relationships with others, my favorite types of conversations, my favorite types of books, my favorite volunteer activities, and my least favorite of these same things. I also looked at my family, my church, and my community. I looked at my favorite causes. *What social issues concern me the most?* I asked. These things furthered my understanding of my story, my *how*, my mission.

Eventually, after significant personal reflection, I concluded that my personal mission is to promote positive change by helping others to make quality decisions personally and in their work-lives (and, as you know, it is now coupled with the vision of becoming an amphitheater for growing God's kingdom).

Why bother with a mission statement? Why bother defining the *how*?

A mission helps throughout our lives, both personally and in our work-lives. One, it helps us know when to say yes and when to say no. Do you want me to volunteer in the kitchen? That's probably not my thing. Do you want me to help out at the pregnancy center, talking to the women who come in seeking help? Maybe that's a fit. Do you want me to speak at your fund-raiser for the pregnancy center? Yes. Maybe someday I'll be an amphitheater for God's kingdom.

A mission statement helps from the job standpoint. It will help when writing a résumé. A solid mission statement will help define which personal or work-related attributes to emphasize. It helps one discern which job and which employer is a better fit. Finding a good match between the job, the employer, and one's mission often spells success and happiness for one's employment future.

A mission statement helps when networking, providing us with a thirty-second sales pitch. A friend noted that she ran into a potential employer at the grocery store. There she was in the middle of the aisle with her shopping cart, with thirty seconds or less to present herself positively to the potential employer. A strong mission statement helps us say what we want to say clearly and succinctly.

Understanding one's mission is also helpful at the interview stage. Imagine that you have been invited to interview in person for a particular job. You are nervous. You hope that the potential employer will realize what a great fit you are for this job. You walk into his office. He invites you to sit down as he starts looking at your application materials. In this brief moment of silence, you speak up, "While we are getting settled, would you mind if I told you a little about myself?" He looks up from the papers on his desk and encourages you to go ahead. (I don't know of anyone who has said no to such a request.) Then you tell him who you are, generally your mission, and how it fits with their stated job needs. You have now told the interviewer the most important thing you wanted him to hear in the interview. With that out of the way, you become more relaxed and focused. You are now ready for his questions.

Finally, and most importantly, God designed each of us in a very special way. He wants us to use the gifts he has given us. It is by understanding these gifts, developing them, and ultimately using them that we will find the path God wants us to follow.

Did you ever give a gift to someone and they didn't acknowledge it with a thank-you? They never said a word to you. Sometime later, you visited their home. You discreetly try to glance around to see if they are using your gift. You don't see it anyplace. As you leave, they direct you to the coat closet and suggest that you find your coat, and they will meet you at the door. There, on the shelf, is your gift. It is still in the box. Your feelings are hurt. You are a little miffed. *If they didn't like it, why didn't they say something? You could have given them the receipt so they could exchange it*, you grumble to yourself.

How do you think God feels when we don't use the many talents and gifts that he has given us? Do you think he could be just a little miffed when we ignore his gifts, or when we don't try to identify the direction that he has planned for us? Self-analysis is critical to discovering the path that God has planned for us. Defining an eternal vision and identifying the *how* within our own stories will put us on a path heading toward God's plan for our lives and our work-lives. We may not get it right the first time, but that's okay. God will speak to each of us along the way, providing further direction each day, each week, and each year.

For we are God's handiwork, created in Christ Jesus to do good works, which God prepared in advance for us to do.
Ephesians 2:10

Reflection & Encouragement

    Vision looks inward and becomes duty.
    Vision looks outward and becomes aspiration.
    Vision looks upward and becomes faith.
    Stephen S. Wise,[13] Rabbi, 1874–1949

Memory Verse

Since, then, you have been raised with Christ,
set your hearts on things above, where Christ is,

---

13 Wise, Stephen S. Satisfaction.com. 2004-2012 Satisfaction.com. July 2, 2012. http://www.satisfaction.com/quotes/author/Stephen_S._Wise

seated at the right hand of God. Set your minds on things above, not on earthly things.

Colossians 3:1–2

Closing Prayer

The closing prayer is from Psalm 119:33–40, as translated in *The Message*.

God, teach me lessons for living, so I can stay the course.

Give me insight, so I can do what you tell me—making my life one long, obedient response.

Guide me down the road of your commandments; I love traveling this freeway!

Give me a bent for your words of wisdom, and not for piling up loot.

Divert my eyes from toys and trinkets, invigorate me on the pilgrim way.

Affirm your promises to me—promises made to all who fear you.

Deflect the harsh words of my critics—but what you say is always so good.

See how hungry I am for your counsel; preserve my life through your righteous ways!

In Jesus' name I pray. Amen.

Make It Personal

Reading material is only somewhat useful. Applying what you have read brings the material to life. The following questions will help you to apply the main concepts of this chapter to your current work-life situation.

1. Like the corporate world, a quality vision statement and mission statement can help a person discern their path both personally and in their work-life. It helps them decide if a particular job is for them, or when they should feel free to say no when asked to volunteer. It sets direction and parameters.

    a. The author's eternal vision is to be an amphitheater for God's kingdom. Ultimately, she wants to hear the words, "well done, good and faithful servant" when she meets Jesus in heaven one day. Her mission is to promote positive change by helping others make quality choices personally and in their work-lives. Write a short paragraph on how the author's vision and mission are designed to help her keep her sights on God and his kingdom.

    b. Looking at the author's mission statement, identify the jobs from the following list that fit within her mission statement: Assembly line worker, car mechanic, guidance counselor, life coach, airline pilot, chef, attorney, retail sales clerk, or nurse.

    c. Of the jobs that fit within the author's mission statement, which one is most likely to help her reach her vision to be an amphitheater for God's kingdom?

2. Begin to define your personal vision statement. Your vision statement should meet the following criteria:

    a. It is your imagined ultimate destination, an ideal, a dream.

b. It affects God's kingdom, an effect that extends beyond the grave.

c. It is something bigger than you can expect to accomplish by yourself.

d. It is tangible or identifiable in a simple sentence – easy to picture (something to hear, feel, or see). Perhaps there is a metaphor that describes your vision.

3. Now begin to define your mission, the realm in which you will work to reach the vision. This is the *how* in your own story.

   a. List all of your past jobs and all of your past hobbies. List what you liked most in each and why. Look for trends. Is there a common thread?

   b. List the types of relationships within which you most enjoyed working. Note why you liked these.

   c. List the types of work environments in which you felt most comfortable when working. List the work environments you liked least in the past. Note the reasons why you either liked or didn't like these environments.

   d. List any of your special talents or particular personality traits that have a positive influence on those around you.

   e. List your strengths and list things you like to avoid.

4. Looking at the various lists that you have made in response to question 3 above, look for themes or consistent items of interest. Building on the themes or items

of interest, try writing a draft of your personal mission statement, the means with which you might try moving closer to your vision.

5. Pray. Ask the Holy Spirit to open your eyes to the mission God has in mind for you. Pray about this daily.

Remember, defining personal vision and mission statements is not easy. Don't worry if you do not have a fine-tuned statement at this time. It is sufficient to simply start thinking about it. As you continue reading this book, you will gain additional insights into yourself and how those insights might affect your vision and mission statements.

Chapter 6

GOD CALLED

*It's in Christ that we find out who we
are and what we are living for.*
Ephesians 1:11 (MSG)

Vision? Mission? Are they easy concepts? No. You have just begun to think about a vision for your life and your work-life after one simple chapter in a book. You might be thinking, "I have no idea."

Don't fret. God has an idea. He has all of the ideas. He has a plan for your life. He will direct your paths, one step at a time. First he will call you to himself, into relationship with him. Then, he will call you to his plan for your life. Sometimes he will call you to action for a moment in time. Sometimes he will call you toward a specific long-term job. For purposes of this book, we will focus on God's call toward a job or a career direction or a vocation.

God's call comes to each of us in different ways. Pastor David Lyle (the pastor at St. Peter's Lutheran Church, Pawleys Island, South Carolina) said that some people can point to a particular day and time that they heard God calling them to lead a life in service to him. They can describe an epiphany, an "ah-ha" moment, when they could hear God speaking to them loudly and clearly. Pastor Lyle then described how he was called to be a pastor, which did not involve such a moment of revelation. Instead, he had a life filled with positive experiences in church and summer Bible camp that became a natural tug on his heart. The experiences he is able to recall began as early as when he was four years old and continued each year. Then one year while working as a summer Bible camp counselor, a pastor at the camp suggested to him that he might want to consider becoming a pastor himself. Weeks of prayer and meditation followed, during which time he carefully and lovingly sought confirmation as to whether this was the direction in which God was calling him.

I think God begins calling us to find his path for our lives at a very early age as he did with Pastor Lyle, but some of us don't hear him or we don't recognize his whisper. I think that he also calls us to serve him in a variety of ways. Many of us think of God's call as being limited to direct religious or church-related fields such as pastors, priests, missionaries to foreign countries, youth leaders, and men's or women's ministry leaders. Although it is quite likely that God has reached out to the people working in these fields, he also calls the rest of us in our work-lives, whatever and wherever we may be. He calls those who work in the factories, at fast food restaurants, in retail stores, and for major corporations. He calls those who operate their own businesses, work for other employers, manage their homes and families, and attend school. God calls people of all walks of life into a variety of directions. His kingdom is not only within a church building or structure; God's kingdom is everywhere.

We know that men were created to busy themselves with labor, and that no sacrifice is more pleasing to God than when each one attends to his calling and studies well to live for the common good.
John Calvin,[14] French theologian, 1509–1564

---

14 Calvin, John. Quote. *Faith & Work Facts*. By Os Hillman. International Coalition of Workplace Ministries. 2005, ICWM. 02 February 2007. http://www.icwm.net/pages.asp?pageid=203

In retrospect, I believe God was calling me for years before I heard him. I needed God to speak loudly because I did not recognize his whispers. I ignored my natural inclination toward psychology or sociology. I ignored my love of reading, and I ignored my natural intrigue with the abilities of a quality public speaker. Instead I listened intently to worldly teachings about wealth, women's liberation, and the advantages of a career choice in fields that were traditionally male-dominated fields. I didn't know that God's call is about the person I am and the person that he made me to be. I didn't hear his whispers.

Even though I did not hear God's early whispers, God does not give up. God put people and events in my life that would help me to hear him. In hindsight, I can now point to a number of examples in which God was tugging on my heart. Over time, his calls got stronger and stronger. Finally, my heart began to ache, wanting my purpose in life to match God's plan for my life.

The beginnings of my writing and speaking career probably started many years before I actually started writing or speaking. I can see God's hand upon me as far back as college, as he worked with me through my education and work experiences. Concurrently, God also worked on my heart. Even though God had been working with me for a lifetime, I first began to notice God's call to a new path about two and a half years before I started writing my first manuscript. I tell you this not because my story is particularly important, but rather so you can see some of the ways God might use to get one's attention.

In early 2001, I was at a women's retreat near Chicago. It was a wonderful retreat attended by about a thousand women. The keynote speaker was a woman named Verla Gillmor. She described her past work-life in the corporate world and her ultimate decision to leave that world to write and to speak. She authored a book entitled *Reality Check*. Verla's story on how she tuned into God's call on her life was very interesting, one worth reading. Her presentation was entertaining, energetic, and uplifting. I listened to Verla with intrigue and admiration, when suddenly I was overwhelmed with emotion. I began to sob uncontrollably. Tears streamed down my face.

In an attempt to comfort me, my sister whispered, "What is the matter? Can I help?"

"I don't know. All I know is that Verla is living my life. I'm supposed to be writing and speaking. I'm not supposed to work in my job anymore."

"Really?" my sister questioned. "That makes no sense."

"I know," I agreed. I heaved with confusion, conviction, and doubt. What a set of mixed up feelings. God was calling me through an extraordinarily emotional response to an enjoyable and inspirational presentation.

After the retreat, I went home. I had a busy house. Our daughters were in middle school. I had a demanding work schedule. Life was busy. Work was busy. I put aside all of the emotions and feelings I had experienced during the retreat. I continued on my then-current work-life path. Life went on as though nothing unusual had happened. I eventually forgot about Verla. I forgot about my tears. I didn't have time, didn't take time to dig deeper into the message that God was sending through Verla. I was too busy. I never quite connected the idea that God might have been using Verla and the retreat to call me to a new work-life adventure.

Later in 2001, that fateful day in September when terrorists downed passenger planes and used small planes to destroy the World Trade Center in New York and to damage the Pentagon in Washington, D.C. As I watched the news reports with dismay, disbelief, and a sinking feeling as my sense of the world seemed to fade away through a crisis that was unthinkable, I questioned the value of my work and my life.

There must be more than this, I thought. *My work has no value. My work has no redeeming purpose.* God used worldly circumstances to call me to service. God allowed this crisis to break my heart as he whispered my name. But I didn't fully understand.

About two months later, during a message in our church on being a servant of God, I was moved … no, compelled … to pray, "Lord, I don't really understand the concept of being a servant; but I know what an employee is, and I want to be your employee." That prayer felt good. *Yes, God's employee. He'd be the perfect boss,* I thought to myself. Afterward, I learned from my sister that God takes prayers like that very seriously, and she believed that God was going to turn my life upside down. She was dead-on. Talk about change.

God speaks to us through the words of his faithful, whether they are leaders of the church, family members, television evangelists, keynote speakers at retreats, friends, or complete strangers. Yet, when my sister told me that God would change my life, I didn't really believe her. I didn't believe that God would actually mess around with my job, my boss, and all other aspects of my employment. I generally thought that even though we pray, God's answers are vague and spiritual, not concrete and earthly.

I was wrong.

Within weeks of praying about being God's employee, my entire work environment began to change. The changes were hard on me. I found myself in an environment in which I no longer fit. Seemingly overnight, my work environment evolved from a reasonably satisfying and productive place to an unhealthy environment in which success was going to come with significantly greater difficulty, if at all. As my work situation declined, there was nothing that I did or said that made any positive impact on the situation.

Hoping that it was a situation I could still resolve, I prayed for help. Instead of being blessed with a positive work environment, however, I received message after message from other sources and events in my life that I should quit my job. For example, while reading a book written by Max Lucado, a prolific Christian author and pastor, I felt a tug on my heart which seemed to say that my job no longer fit my life's values and priorities. When watching Joyce Meyer on television, she seemed to speak directly to me when she emphasized how we cannot serve both God and money. "You can't be double-minded," she said.

Everywhere I turned, I began to read and hear similar messages. So I looked for other employment opportunities, believing that a new job was my call from God. As I looked, I prayed that God would open the right doors for my life and for his plan for me. No suitable opportunities presented themselves. I thought that God was not answering my prayers.

I was wrong again. He was answering. He was calling. I was not listening. I still did not fully recognize his voice.

Confused, I continued to pray for guidance. "Dear God," I would pray, "I believe that you want me to quit my job. Yet you haven't provided a new job for me. I'm not sure I'm hearing you correctly. Please be clearer with me." The messages continued as the months went by. *You can't be double-minded. You cannot serve both God and money. You have a different purpose.*

"No one can serve two masters. Either you will hate the one and love the other, or you will be devoted to the one and despise the other. You cannot serve both God and money."
Jesus, Matthew 6:24

The more time that went by, the more frustration I felt because I was not able to resolve my negative work-life situation. I tried everything to improve the situation, but with no results. Work consumed more and more of my time until I had no time for my family. Months had gone by and I was exhausted. "God, what is it you want me to do?" I silently screamed in prayer. "You haven't opened any new doors for me; yet you seem to be telling me to quit my job. Quitting makes no sense. That would be illogical. Everyone knows not to quit a job before getting a new one. God, make it more clear to me. I'm not smart enough to figure this out on my own." I boldly demanded his answer.

Then, for three weeks straight, night after night after night, I dreamed about ways to quit my job. In one dream, I stormed out of work in a huff. In another dream, I refused to get out of bed. In another, I quietly packed up my things and slipped out the door. It was like that song by Paul Simon entitled, *Fifty Ways to Leave Your Lover*. But in this case I dreamed of twenty-one ways to leave my job. "Just slip out the back, Jack …," so state the lyrics in Paul Simon's song. During a pleasant meeting with my boss at the end of the third week, we jointly agreed to eliminate my job. God spoke to me through dreams. He changed my circumstances so that I had little or no other choice but to acquiesce. Yet I still didn't understand what he wanted me to do.

"If a person is ever going to do anything worthwhile, there will be times when he must risk everything by his leap in the dark. In the spiritual realm, Jesus Christ demands that you risk everything you hold on to or believe through common sense, and leap by faith into what He says." Oswald Chambers.[15] Scottish Christian minister, 1874–1917

---

15 Taken from *My Utmost for His Highest* by Oswald Chambers, edited by James Reimann, © 1992 by Oswald Chambers Publications Assn., Ltd., and used by permission of Discovery House Publisher, Grand Rapids, MI 49501. All rights reserved.

More than eighteen months had passed since I first asked God to allow me to be his employee. Two and a half years had passed since I heard Verla Gillmor speak. I was now on a new path. But it wasn't until I finally gave up my security blankets, my job and my pay, that God revealed to me his plan for my next step.

"Write," he said, as he typed a table of contents in my mind.

Although I asked to be God's employee, when God called and invited me to work for him, I fought him every step of the way.

God spoke to me in a variety of ways, calling me to him and calling me into service for him. He called me to change my career direction, my job, my pay, and my expectations for pay. God spoke, but I didn't recognize his voice. God spoke, but I was too busy to hear him. God spoke, but his direction didn't make sense to me. God spoke, but his instructions seemed incomplete. God spoke, but I needed assurances, clarity, and convincing evidence that it was really him. His call was clear and he made sure that I would not miss it, not this time. But since I did not understand it and could not accept it, God chose to make it clearer and clearer and clearer, until I finally said, "Yes, I am listening."

A hurricane wind ripped through the mountains and shattered the rocks before God, but God wasn't to be found in the wind; after the wind an earthquake, but God wasn't in the earthquake; and after the earthquake fire, but God wasn't in the fire; and after the fire a gentle and quiet whisper.
1 Kings 19:11–12 (MSG)

It is important to carefully evaluate our changing circumstances or our feelings to avoid responding impulsively, believing that we have heard God's whisper. It is important to be certain that it is God calling. Jesus told his disciples that if we know Jesus as our shepherd and our Savior, we will recognize his voice. Specifically, Jesus said, *The gatekeeper opens the gate for him, and the sheep listen to his voice. He calls his own sheep by name and leads them out. When he has brought out all his own, he goes on ahead of them, and his sheep follow him because they know his voice. But they will never follow a stranger; in fact, they will run away from him because they do not recognize a stranger's voice* (John 10:3–5).

Samuel, a boy dedicated by his mother to serving God, was not accustomed to hearing God's voice. So when God called Samuel by name in the middle of the night, Samuel thought the calls he heard were from Eli, the priest who was raising him. The Bible tells us that it was not common at that time for God to speak directly to individuals. It was the first time that Samuel heard God calling to him, so he didn't recognize God's voice. But Eli figured it out and told Samuel that the voice he heard was God's. The following is an excerpt from the Bible telling Samuel's story:

> *"The boy Samuel was serving God under Eli's direction. This was at a time when the revelation of God was rarely heard or seen. One night Eli was sound asleep (his eyesight was very bad—he could hardly see). It was well before dawn; the sanctuary lamp was still burning. Samuel was still in bed in the Temple of God, where the Chest of God rested.*
>
> *Then God called out, "Samuel, Samuel!"*
>
> *Samuel answered, "Yes? I'm here." Then he ran to Eli saying, "I heard you call. Here I am."*
>
> *Eli said, "I didn't call you. Go back to bed." And so he did.*
>
> *God called again, "Samuel, Samuel!"*

> *Samuel got up and went to Eli, "I heard you call. Here I am."*
>
> *Again Eli said, "Son, I didn't call you. Go back to bed." (This all happened before Samuel knew God for himself. It was before the revelation of God had been given to him personally.)*
>
> *God called again, "Samuel!"— the third time! Yet again Samuel got up and went to Eli, "Yes? I heard you call me. Here I am."*
>
> *That's when it dawned on Eli that God was calling the boy. So Eli directed Samuel, "Go back and lie down. If the voice calls again, say, 'Speak, God. I'm your servant, ready to listen.'" Samuel returned to his bed.*
>
> *Then God came and stood before him exactly as before, calling out, "Samuel! Samuel!"*
>
> *Samuel answered, "Speak. I'm your servant, ready to listen."*
> 1 Samuel 3:1–10 (MSG)

Sometimes when God calls us, we might not realize that it is God calling. Perhaps we have not heard God in the past. Perhaps we are not accustomed to listening for God's call. However, like Samuel, we can seek the advice of others (pastors, priests, mature Christians, and other church leaders) to help us discern whether the prompting we feel or the voice we hear or the message we sense is truly from God.

In addition to seeking wise counsel from others, we may want to follow Samuel's lead to further discern God's call. Once Samuel understood that God was calling him, he told God he was ready to listen. We too can tell God that we are ready to listen. We can spend more time in prayer, both asking God to help us to hear him and pausing in time of reflection, using the ears of our heart to listen for his response. We can also listen by reading the Bible. It is called the

Living Word because, with the help of the Holy Spirit, the Bible can speak to us today about whatever is on our heart. If God wants you to hear something specific, he will bless you with the ability to hear through his Spirit. Opening and reading the Bible is another way to listen. Regularly seek to hear God by drawing closer to him through prayer, Bible study, and worship. God will draw closer to you. Eventually, you will be close enough to God that you will not only hear him calling your name, but you will hear his gentle whisper in whatever manner he chooses to speak to you.

God speaks to some people directly, such as in the way he called Samuel as a voice in the night, or in the way he spoke to Moses, appearing to him as a burning bush. God will speak through dreams as when he spoke to Joseph through a dream about twelve sheaves of grain. Sometimes God's message comes through angels, as when Mary was told that she was chosen to be the mother of Jesus. But most of us will not receive direct messages from God. In many cases, God simply places us in the situation, providing wisdom and skills as needed and when needed, directly or through godly advisors. This is how God called and used Esther.

Esther, a Jewish girl, did not hear directly from God any particular message about his will for her in her particular circumstances. But she found herself in a position of influence as the queen to King Xerxes.

When King Xerxes banished his first queen from his sight for being disobedient, he issued an order to bring all beautiful young virgins to the palace so he might find a new queen. Esther, an orphan who was raised by her cousin Mordecai, was one of the young women brought to the palace.

Esther spent about a year in the king's harem, being prepared to meet the king and to potentially become queen. During this time, she learned her lessons well. Even though this was highly unusual and likely not part of her life dream (as she was separated from her family and friends), Esther learned all that she was supposed to learn, and, based on the advice of Mordecai, she also kept her nationality and family background a secret. When she was finally brought before King Xerxes, he was so impressed with Esther that he made her his queen (Esther 1–2).

Sometime later, based on the advice of one of the king's nobles, King Xerxes issued a decree to destroy the entire Jewish population. Mordecai informed Esther of the decree and urged her to plead with the king for mercy for her people, the Jews. Esther initially said no, fearing she would be put to death for approaching the king without an invitation. However, Mordecai strongly suggested to Esther that she may have been placed in this highly unusual and influential position, as queen, even though she was Jewish, just for this reason: to save the Jewish people (Esther 3:8–4:16).

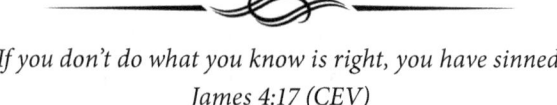

If you don't do what you know is right, you have sinned.
James 4:17 (CEV)

Ultimately, after prayer, fasting, and careful planning, Esther approached the king. He extended his scepter, thereby sparing her life, even though she approached without an invitation. Taking a careful, respectful, and honorable approach (one which she likely learned while in the harem), Esther was able to positively influence the king, and he then issued a new decree, enabling the Jews to protect themselves. Esther's bravery and cautious approach saved all of her people from destruction. (See Esther chapters 5 through 8.)

God called Esther. He placed her in an unlikely situation, taught her how to present herself and her wishes to the king, advised her through her cousin Mordecai, and remained with her as she answered his call by doing what was necessary for God's kingdom, even at the risk of her own life.

Be very careful, then, how you live—not as unwise but as wise, making the most of every opportunity, because the days are evil. Therefore do not be foolish, but understand what the Lord's will is.
Ephesians 5:15–17

Perhaps, you too will find yourself in an unusual position or in an unwanted work-life situation. Follow Esther's example. Do the best you can. Learn as much as you can. God may have placed you in this situation for a purpose. Perhaps the situation will lead to an opportunity to do something particularly good for God's kingdom. Perhaps God placed you in this situation to learn something that will be needed for another day and another time. While in this situation, listen for his voice. Seek him through prayer and fasting.

When looking for new employment, as previously stated, it is most helpful to have a vision and a mission. However, God's call on your life may not clearly fit your vision or mission. If he places you in an unexpected situation or calls you in an unexpected manner, pray for wisdom and understanding. Keep close to him to help you hear his whisper. Seek the advice of wise and godly people. Maybe God is speaking through them. Finally, do the good you know you are called to do. Just maybe, your mission for this one day or for this particular period in your life is to do the good you are called to do in this place, at this time, until God opens a new door or opens your eyes to a new vision or mission.

Reflection & Encouragement

"If I am united with Jesus Christ, I hear God all the time through the devotion of hearing. A flower, a tree, or a servant of God may convey God's message to me. What hinders me from hearing is my attention to other things. It is not that I don't want to hear God, but I am not devoted in the right areas of my life. I am devoted to things and even to service and my own convictions. God may say whatever He wants, but I just don't hear Him. The attitude of a child of God should always be, 'Speak, for Your servant hears.' If I have not developed and nurtured this devotion of hearing, I can only hear God's voice at certain times. At other times I become deaf to Him because my attention is to other things – things which I think I must do. This is not living the life of a child of God. Have you heard God's voice today?"

Oswald Chambers,
Scottish Christian minister, 1874–1917[16]

Memory Verse

Come to me with your ears wide open.
Listen, and you will find life.
Isaiah 55:3 (NLT)

Closing Prayer

Dear Father, thank you for having patience with me, and forgive me for not listening with my whole heart for your call on my life. As your servant Samuel said, "Speak. I'm ready to listen," I too want to hear you

---

16 Taken from *My Utmost for His Highest* by Oswald Chambers, edited by James Reimann, © 1992 by Oswald Chambers Publications Assn., Ltd., and used by permission of Discovery House Publisher, Grand Rapids, MI 49501. All rights reserved.

and I am ready to listen. Please, count me worthy of your calling; grant me your power, such that I may fulfill every good purpose and every act as prompted by faith in you. I pray this so that the name of my Lord Jesus may be glorified by the manner in which I live. This is all possible through the grace of my Lord, Jesus Christ, for whom I am eternally grateful. Amen. (Adapted in part from 2 Thessalonians 1:11–12.)

Make It Personal

Reading material is only somewhat useful. Applying what you have read brings the material to life. The following questions will help you to apply the main concepts of this chapter to your current work-life situation.

1. Imagine a small child comes to you with a secret. She cups her tiny hands around your ear and whispers. You can feel her warm, moist breath as she talks. Sometimes, God's call is a simple whisper.

    a. Drawing close enough to God in order to hear his whisper is a lot like making a new friend. What are some things you might do when trying to make a new friend?

    b. Try to translate the list you came up with from question 1.a. above into ways to build a closer relationship with God. For example, when trying to make a new friend, you might spend time talking with them. This would compare with praying to God and listening for his response.

2. Think about your life history and make a timeline of significant choices, changes, and learning experiences. Ask yourself if any of these choices or changes might

be used by God for his kingdom purposes, for a special assignment that he has in mind for you.

3. Identify godly people in your life with whom you could consult if you are trying to discern whether you are hearing from God or not.

4. Esther was in a complicated situation, one that most likely did not fit any vision for her life she had ever imagined. Sometimes we will find our current situations are just as complicated. Seeing how our current situation fits into the ultimate puzzle of life might not be immediately possible. Think about Esther's response in her circumstance. Is your position just as confusing as hers? Following her lead as an example, consider what you might do to make the best out of your current situation.

5. You may have had a vision and a mission for your work-life, but due to unwanted job loss, your previous vision and/or your mission seems destroyed. This is an opportunity to listen anew to God's call on your life.

    a. Thank God for new opportunities to hear his call and opportunities to discover his plan for the next step in your work-life.

    b. Through prayer, seek God's voice; ask for the ability to hear his call; seek wisdom to understand his plan for your work-life in this trying time.

CHAPTER 7

WHEN IN DOUBT, START WITH HIS COMMAND

But be very careful to keep the commandment and the law that Moses the servant of the Lord gave you: to love the LORD your God, to walk in obedience to him, to keep his commands, to hold fast to him and to serve him with all your heart and all your soul.
Joshua 22:5

You may be asking, "What does God call us to do? I don't know that I've heard him calling me."

I remember when our first daughter was born and it was time to leave the hospital with her. I am the type of person who gets out the operating instructions before plugging in my new television. So when the hospital gave us our baby and congratulated us and sent us on our way, I couldn't help but wonder, *Where are the operating instructions?* The baby came with no instructions. How was I going to know what to do or when to do it? "Oh, you'll be fine," my mother said. "You'll know what to do. The baby will tell you." The baby didn't speak English.

Not a problem. In time, I learned to recognize her cries. I knew when she was hungry or if she needed changing. I knew if she was uncomfortable or if she was happy. In time, I learned to read her signals most of the time. When I didn't understand, I would try doing a variety of things until I got it right.

Pursuing God's plan for our work-lives may be a little like trying to understand a newborn baby. God has provided us with many insights into his plan, and it is our job to tune in to his message. For each of us the message will be different because, for each of us, God has a specific plan. God gave each of us different skills, abilities, and passions. He placed each of us in different work-life situations. *There are different kinds of spiritual gifts, but the same Spirit is the source of them all. There are different kinds of service, but we serve the same Lord. God works in different ways, but it is the same God who does the work in all of us* (1 Corinthians 12:4–6 NLT).

God has been speaking to you. Perhaps you have not begun to read his signals. Start with the words of Jesus. He said in Mark 12:30–31 that the most important thing is to *Love the LORD your God with all your heart and with all your soul and with all your mind and with all your strength*. The second is this: *Love your neighbor as yourself*. In seeking to live this out, I refer to a quote from the book, *A Life Worth Leading*.[17] *You honor God by being true to the way God has created you. By using your gifts, abilities, passions, and desires to make a difference in the world, you are answering God's call on your life*. And remember, 'whatever you do whether in word or deed, do it all in the name of the Lord Jesus, giving thanks to God the Father through him' (Colossians 2:6; 3:17).

Thus far, we have talked about having a foundation of strength in Christ Jesus rather than in ourselves; having an eternal vision, a vision that goes beyond our dream job or our retirement, a vision set on heavenly things; pursuing our vision within our own story, our

---

17 Burtness, Eric. *A Life Worth Leading*. Minneapolis, MN: Augsburg Fortress, 2006 Augsburg Fortress. 70.

mission; and tuning in to God's call. In the classic career model, we may pursue our vision through building blocks of education, passions, and personality traits. The biblical career model is similar.

Imagine the structure of a house. There are building blocks, four columns as pillars of strength upon which to build one's work-life direction and upon which we may find God's plan for our work-lives. These pillars are based upon the greatest commandment: Love the Lord with all of our heart, soul, mind, and strength. These pillars of strength are an indication of God's call on our lives. God expects us to use these in ways that love him and love those around us.

*So if you faithfully obey the commands I am giving you today—
to love the LORD your God and to serve him with all your heart
and with all your soul then I will send rain on your land in its
season, both autumn and spring rains, so that you may gather
in your grain, new wine and olive oil. I will provide grass in the
fields for your cattle, and you will eat and be satisfied.
Deuteronomy 11:13–15*

Love the Lord with All Your Heart
When our oldest daughter was graduating from high school, I told her that I was so proud of her, and I thanked her for being a truly responsible teenager. "I really appreciate everything about you," I told her. "I could always trust you. I knew where you were and what you were doing and who you were with. You always came home on time or called to let me know if you'd be late. Thank you for being you."

"I learned that from you, Mom," she replied.

Wow. Really? I thought to myself, my heart filling with self-pride. I couldn't wait to hear more. "What did I do that influenced you so?"

I asked, looking forward to hearing about some sort of wisdom I had passed on.

"Well," she simply said, "you were always late when you picked me up after your work. It made me worry, and I never wanted to make you worry like that."

My prideful heart was instantly dropped into its rightful place.

I didn't mean to be late all of the time. I tried so hard to be on time. So frequently, though, I'd check the time and discover that I had about a half hour before it was time to leave. So I'd start working on the next project. I'd start researching or writing, drafting the next document, or revising a prior draft. I'd find a related article and find myself digging deeper and deeper into the content, fascinated by its application to my work. I loved doing legal work. I loved researching. I loved writing with a purpose, massaging the chosen words to get the precise result.

Suddenly, after losing all track of time, I'd come back to the world of parental responsibility, check the time and race out to my car. *I'm late again.* I'd silently chastise myself. *What am I going to tell Chelsy this time?* Of course, when you are running late, every stoplight is red, there is a long slow train at the tracks, and there is a police officer with radar at every turn. I wasn't just late. I was extremely late.

It still happens to me. Not only do I lose track of the time, I can get so caught up in my research, my reading, or my writing that I can forget entire appointments. I've had to place notes in the center of my laptop screen to keep me on task. Luckily for me, 3M invented those little yellow sticky notes. I love what I am doing. I am doing exactly what God has planned for me at this point in my life.

Love the Lord your God with all your heart. The first set of building blocks in our work-life structure, lifting up from our foundation in Christ, is passion. God gave us a sense of passion to guide us in the direction he has planned for our lives. We may have passion for a hobby, passion for a charitable or political cause, or passion for a type of work. God wants us to follow our passions in ways that honor him, because it is our passions that lead us to the job God has planned for us.

Nehemiah was a man of passion. When his brother reported to him that the people of Jerusalem were struggling and that the city's walls and doors were destroyed, he sat down and wept. Then for days he mourned and fasted. Nehemiah was passionate for the Israelites and for Jerusalem, and it hurt him to the core to know of their struggles. He prayed. He prayed for success, having decided to request the king's permission to go to Jerusalem. He needed permission because he was the king's cupbearer. The following spring, Nehemiah received the king's permission to return to Jerusalem and rebuild the city.

Following Nehemiah's arrival in Jerusalem, and after surveying the situation, much work with much help was begun. Amazing progress was being made until a number of their enemies discovered what they were doing and planned to attack them. Nehemiah and the many workers, with the help of God, guarded the city and derailed the enemies' plans. From that point forward, they continued to do the work, but now with weapons in one hand and guards stationed around them, with a plan to blast trumpets in the event of trouble. Now prepared for enemy attack, they worked day and night with passion. By fall, the work was completed (Nehemiah 1-6).

A man of passion, Nehemiah was filled with love for Jerusalem. He was a man who could not be stopped, even with the threat of enemy attack. His passion was shared and felt by the many people working with him. Through his passion, Nehemiah found himself doing the job God had planned for him.

As we try to define our mission, as we question what God has planned for our lives and our work-lives, we need to look closely at our passions.

Many people find themselves questioning what God has planned for their work-lives. When leaving high school, young students question whether they should get additional education or begin working. They often don't know what kind of work they would be interested in doing, and they can't imagine doing any particular type of work for the rest of their lives. It is hard enough to think about next year or the next five years, let alone trying to plan for a lifetime. Often they are not ready to select a career direction, simply because they have not had enough life experiences to know who they are or what field of work will strike their hearts with passion.

Mid-career folks often start to question whether their job is as good as it is going to get. They might face disappointment as they reach the conclusion that the dream job they had envisioned is likely unattainable. They sometimes find that they got into their current employment situation out of convenience. They might be comfortable, but each day they envision greener grass on the other side of the fence. Each day they ask themselves, *what if...* as they dream of their ultimate passions, their hobbies, or their ideal job. Often they find themselves saying to a friend, "If I could just find a way to make a living doing that."

Many people entering that seventh inning stretch of life, looking at retirement but not ready to quit being productive in some manner, say to their friends and family, "Now I can afford to do the job that I always wanted to do." Or they might dig into the hobbies they always loved but never had enough time to do. Or they might finally find the time to volunteer for an organization that supports their favorite charitable or political cause.

God has a plan for each of our lives. He planted desires in our hearts, passions within our souls, interests that capture our attention, enthusiasm for certain causes, and purposeful love. By instilling such desires, passions, interests, and enthusiasm, God is directing each of us toward the plan he has for our lives. He made us to care deeply about certain things, albeit not all the same things. He made each of us with a sense of joy or comfort in a particular environment or with a particular activity or in pursuit of a particular cause. Our passions serve to define our purpose. There is great joy when our work is built upon our passions. In Ecclesiastes 3:22, we read, *So I saw that there is nothing better for a person than to enjoy their work, because that is their lot.*

Our oldest daughter is like the pied piper with young children. She loves everyone she meets. Each child is adorable to her and has a particularly special trait she can identify. Our daughter also has enough energy to power an entire town, if it were possible to convert her personal energy into electrical energy. God gave her a passion for athletics, for an active lifestyle, and for fun. She knows that it is through these passions she will find God's plan for her life.

Our youngest daughter is an artist. She doodles with crayons, making beautiful flowers. She sketches with pencil, creating a drawing of an item of clothing, giving each fold of the fabric a touchable quality. She has an eye for what matches, what complements, what softens, and what pops. God gave her a passion for design. It is this passion that will help her find God's plan for her life.

If our daughters focus on these passions, I am certain God will open the doors that will take them into a work-life adventure designed just for them, a work-life adventure that will place each of them in position to best serve God's overall purpose at each point in time.

What do you love to do? What do you do that causes you to lose all track of time? What possibly happens in your day that causes you to forget about all other appointments or obligations? In what environments are you most comfortable? Do you love to be outdoors? Are you energized by listening to or playing music, by reading, by solving puzzles, by finding solutions to a problem, by helping others, or by participation in a particular sport? What drives you to act with intensity, with focus, with deliberation, or deep attentiveness? What causes you to work with fervor? What causes you to lose all track of time, making you late to your appointments or forgetting about them entirely?

Answering these questions will help you to identify your passions and know what excites your heart. Develop your passions.

Experiment a little. Try new endeavors. Like it? Pursue it. Guard it. God gave you these desires so that you will be drawn toward the work he has planned for you.

Guard your heart above all else,
for it determines the course of your life.
Proverbs 4:23 (NLT)

Know who you are. Know who God made you to be. Know your heart. It is the first step toward a work-life adventure too great to miss, an adventure defined for you by God himself. *Do not put out the Spirit's fire* (1 Thessalonians 5:19 NIV 1984). The fire within comes from God. Recognize it. Build on it. It is a critical part of your mission, the *how* in your own story for pursuing an eternal vision.

Love the Lord with All Your Soul

A friend and I were talking about how things have changed over the years, how people knew each other, cared for each other, and forgave certain behaviors that were not intended to be harmful. In this conversation, she told me a story of her father, who had owned a grocery store in a small town when she was a child.

It was a small store in a small town. Her father knew almost every customer, where they lived and how they lived, whether they were needy or whether they managed comfortably. One of the customers would come to the store almost daily. As he shopped for the several small items he needed each day, he would wander slowly throughout the aisles of groceries. As he passed the produce, he would help himself to a banana or an apple. He would take the fruit and eat it as he slowly walked around the store, finishing the item just as he'd arrive at the next section of the store, such as the baked goods section. There he might find a roll or a bun. Again, he would help himself and wander around the store a little longer. He basically ate his way around the entire store, until he had finished one small meal. Then he would pay for a couple items that he carried to his home.

My friend's father, the store owner, knew this customer and knew that he ate his way around the store. He also understood the man's financial circumstances. He never stopped the man, and he never turned him over to the police. This unspoken act of kindness was never acknowledged by the customer with a thank you or with a promise to pay in the future, but the practice of eating his way around the store continued for years.

Finally, several days had passed and the customer had not shown up at the store. The owner began to worry about him and finally called the police, not to report the almost-daily minor theft, but to report that the customer was missing. The police went to the man's home and found that he had died alone, sitting in a chair. He had been there for a few days. In the home they found a will. The customer had left his entire estate, meager as it was, to the store owner.

Love the Lord your God with all of your soul. Love is a verb, an action word. We show our love by the things we do and the ways we act. We show our love for the Lord our God by the way we treat others around us, the way we behave around others, and the way we pursue our work. Our soul is our emotional self, our moral self, our thoughts, feelings, and our nature. Our soul is who we are apart from our physical being. Our soul in the work-life context comprises our character traits, our personal values, our work-related values, our work ethic, and our behaviors or behavioral skills.

Can you see into the store owner's soul by looking at the way he treated this customer, the customer who, out of personal need, ate his way through the store almost every day? I see a man who exhibited kindness, courtesy, patience, love, compassion, generosity, hospitality, and consideration. Perhaps you can see more. I see a man who loved God with all his soul and such love was evident in the way he treated this customer.

The Bible identifies many desirable character traits. These include faithfulness, goodness, the ability to exercise self-control, perseverance, godliness, kindness, the ability to show love (2 Peter 1:5–7), mercy, generosity, fairness (Psalm 112:5–6), humility, gentleness, patience, tolerance, supportiveness forgiveness, peaceful, thankfulness (Colossians 3:12–16), and righteousness (Romans 14:17).

A person who loves God with all his soul looks out for the good of others (1 Corinthians 10:24), looks to the interests of others (Philippians 2:4), is devoted to others in brotherly love, honors others above himself, zealously serves the Lord, is joyful in hope, patient in affliction, faithful in prayer, shares with God's people who are in need, hospitable, blesses others, rejoices with others, mourns with others, lives harmoniously with others, is willing to associate with persons of lower position, does what is right, and lives at peace with others to the extent that it depends on him (Romans 12:10–19).

I often learn many lessons by observing my husband Wayne. In every story he tells involving another person, he notes that the person is a really nice person and a good friend. He finds the good in everyone. He takes time to meet and chat with those working in service positions, whether they are working as a cashier, a receptionist, wait-staff, or at similar jobs, making sure that he treats them respectfully and, more importantly, appreciates the work they do. Wayne is Wayne. The person you meet is the person behind the face. He has no hidden agenda. He is reliable and trustworthy. He is a man who knows his soul and is true to himself in all that he does.

Know your soul. Identify and build upon your godly character traits. Use such traits in your work-life, whether you are a store owner, teacher, laborer, construction worker, or machinist.

All companies, all employers, and all managers have their own set of character traits and values. Some companies try to instill a set of common character traits and values among their employees by defining them as shared values, training employees on the values and managing performance against such values. If your character traits and values are inconsistent with those of your employer, manager, or company, you will likely find it very difficult to be successful or happy in that employment situation.

Know your character traits. Know your values. Know your soul and be true to yourself, not only in your personal life but also in your work-life. Find work, employment, or a manager who appreciates and fosters your godly character traits and values, so you will be able to love the Lord your God with all your soul in your daily work.

For the kingdom of God is not a matter of eating and drinking, but of righteousness, peace and joy in the Holy Spirit, because anyone who serves Christ in this way is pleasing to God and receives human approval.
Romans 14:17–18

Love the Lord with All Your Strength
Ecclesiastes 9:10 says, *Whatever your hand finds to do, do it with all your might.*

Frankly, I'm not very strong. I'm quite a wimp actually. I never could throw a softball more than twenty feet. But I've learned to compensate with leverage. My husband is amazed at the way I can move the furniture around the house when I decide it would look better in another location. Then if you add just the right equipment or tools, there seems to be no limit to what I can move around the house.

Our oldest daughter is a gymnast. Now that is a sport that requires full body strength. I recall one time when she was still in high school and I went to wake her up for school. She was lying on her stomach, so I reached to rub her back. I expected to feel the relaxed softness of sleeping muscles. Instead, her back muscles were as hard as a tabletop, even at rest. She is all muscle. I'm certain there is not an ounce of fat on her entire body.

Love the Lord with all your strength. Do your work with all your might. In this context, the words *might* and *strength* have broader meanings than muscle power. They also include emotional toughness, force, effectiveness, realm of influence, persuasive power, vigor, vitality, drive, heartiness, energy, and gusto. Strength and might may include physical and mental ability, capability, competence, aptitude, skill, qualifications, wherewithal, resources, giftedness, talent, ability to learn, and fitness.

Love the Lord with all your physical and mental ability, your talent, your energy, and your influence. It's a big calling. We influence everyone we encounter and everyone who sees us, even when we don't notice them.

Jesus told his disciples a parable about a man who was going on a journey. Before he left, he called his servants together and gave them each a number of talents. In Jesus' time, a talent was a form of money that was worth more than a thousand dollars in today's money. He gave one servant five talents, another servant two talents, and the last servant only one talent. Jesus explained that each servant received an amount according to his ability. The man's expectation was that each servant would invest the talents and return the money with the profits to the man upon his return.

When the man returned from his journey, he sought out his servants and requested his money. The servant with five talents had invested wisely and gave the man ten talents in return. The servant with two talents also invested wisely and gave the man four talents in return. The master was very pleased with these two servants and said to each of them, *Well done, good and faithful servant! You have been faithful with a few things; I will put you in charge of many things. Come and share your master's happiness!* (Matthew 25:21, 23).

The last servant hid his talent, making no investment on behalf of the man. So he was able to return only the one talent. The man was very angry with the last servant. He called him lazy and wicked, and said, *Take the talent from him and give it to the one who has the ten talents. For everyone who has will be given more, and he will have an abundance. Whoever does not have, even what he has will be taken from him* (Matthew 25:28–29, NIV 1984).

We too have been given many talents. While the talents in the parable were in the form of money, this parable translates well into talents in the form of strength and might. We have each been given certain physical and mental abilities, energies, and areas of influence. We each have certain capabilities, fields of competence, aptitude levels, and skills. Applying the parable to our lives today, we have been given these talents to invest for our master, our Lord, our God.

Love the Lord your God with all your strength. Love is a verb, a word requiring action. To love God with all our strength means that we are to honor him by using all of our abilities, skills, and influence in our lives and in our work-lives. Use all abilities, skills, and influence to love the Lord. Use them completely. Use them for God and his kingdom, and you too will one day hear the words the man said to his first two servants, "Well done."

In the parable, each servant was given a different quantity of talents. That is true for each of us as well. We each have different abilities, different skills, different degrees of influence, and different aptitude levels. Our differences were intentional, because we each have a different purpose in life. We each have a different job to do.

We have different gifts, according to the grace given to each of us. If your gift is prophesying, then prophesy in accordance with your faith; if it is serving, then serve; if it is teaching, then teach; if it is to encourage, then give encouragement; if it is giving, then give generously; if it is to lead, do it diligently; if it is to show mercy, do it cheerfully.
Romans 12:6–8

If you fully understand your abilities, skills, realms of influence, and aptitude to learn more, and if you apply these things in your work-life, a work-life that honors God, you will be taking a step toward the plan God has for you. If you use your skills and abilities in a field that matches your passions and interests in life, in a working environment that corresponds with your personal character traits, then you will be well on your way toward a work-life adventure of your dreams, an adventure too great to miss, a future designed by God himself.

Know who you are. Understand your heart, your soul, and your strength. Seek to combine these into a work-life direction that honors God. Honorable work is honest, morally upright, principled, decent, good, and ethical. Honorable work may serve God either directly or indirectly. It may serve others either directly or indirectly. Honorable work can be found in most professions, whether you are an administrative assistant, an accountant, a road worker, a plumber, a bus driver, a computer operator, a photographer, or a manager. The list of honorable jobs is nearly endless.

Some of you might be wondering just how your current employment situation could possibly be serving God. I don't think we have to worry about that. Sometimes our work is only part of the picture. Maybe our work serves God's purpose ultimately in combination with the work of another person. According to the apostle Paul in 1 Corinthians 3:8, *The one who plants and the one who waters have one purpose, and they will each be rewarded according to their own labor.*

Maybe our work is a mere stepping stone to the ultimate purpose that God has planned. I wasn't always an author. In fact, in college I avoided all writing classes, taking only the minimum required classes that involved writing. I recall staying awake half the night trying to write, in longhand, a single-page essay. Over and over and over I started, struggling to complete three short paragraphs. I worked hard, but my grade reflected my ability rather than my effort. Not so good. Ultimately, after graduating from law school, I accepted a job as an intellectual property attorney. In this job, exceptional writing skills were critical. I'll tell you more about this story later. Suffice it to say that I had a patient boss who was willing to invest in training. Eventually I caught on.

I had an aptitude to learn, and God used that job to teach me things I would need for the work that he had planned for me. Working as an intellectual property lawyer was not God's long-term purpose for me. The work I was doing served my employer. There was no direct or obvious tie between that job and serving God. In hindsight, however, I know that writing patent applications served God's purpose by preparing me for the work I do today.

God has been doing this sort of thing for people for hundreds of years. Just think about Moses, as one example. When God wanted Moses to confront Pharaoh and gain freedom for the Israelites, Moses didn't think he was qualified for the job. Moses argued with God, pleading with him to send someone else. Moses believed he was a poor speaker. *Moses said to the LORD, "Pardon your servant, Lord, I have never been eloquent, neither in the past nor since you have spoken to your servant. I am slow of speech and tongue." The LORD said to him, "Who gave human beings their mouths? Who makes them deaf or mute? Who gives them sight or makes them blind? Is it not I, the LORD? Now go; I will help you speak and will teach you what to say"* (Exodus 4:10–12). God basically told Moses, "Hey, I am the one who gives skills and talents to all people. So I will give you the skill and talent you need, when you need it, for the job that I want you to do."

Some of us worry that we might not pick the career God wants for us. Instead of worrying about that point, we can pray about it. We can ask God to help us make a career choice that is along the path he has planned for us. He will guide us if we ask. If we misunderstand his direction and choose a path different than God's plan, he will use the opportunity for good and then move us. Like I said,

I was an intellectual property lawyer, and God used the opportunity to train me for his purpose for my life at this time. After working for that company for nearly ten years, God nudged me along into a new opportunity. He continued to move me from one job to the next, molding me, teaching me, and training me. Finally, it was time for me to hear him calling me to write.

God had a plan for me. In spite of my plans, my work-life choices, my personal dreams, and my choices, God took hold of me and put me on the path of his choosing. Because of that, I am convinced that we simply need to love him to the fullest by using the strength and might he gave us, in the best way we can possibly understand. God will then move us where he wants us.

We don't have to know his plan. We don't have to worry about being right. We simply need to love him with all our heart, our soul, and our strength. God will take it from there.

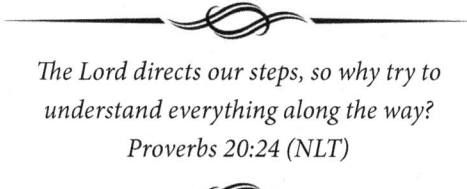

The Lord directs our steps, so why try to understand everything along the way?
Proverbs 20:24 (NLT)

Love the Lord with All Your Mind

Love the Lord with all your mind. Our mind includes our intelligence, our ability to think and reason, our sense of judgment, knowledge, and wisdom. It includes what is known as common sense as well as knowledge gained through education, training, and experience. God gave us our intellectual abilities and our abilities to reason, and we are to develop and use these abilities out of love for him.

Just like talents, God gave these abilities to each of us in varying degrees. Some of us find the sciences easy to learn. Others have an aptitude for mathematical logic, the written word, mechanical technologies, or electrical engineering. For some, one ability of the mind is near genius, while other abilities of the mind are limited. For others, our intellectual abilities are well-rounded, with no particular ability standing out above the rest.

Some of us prefer to learn by reading, some prefer to learn by watching, and some prefer to learn by doing. Although we each have a different aptitude for learning, every one of us can increase our knowledge in a wide variety of ways. We can pursue additional education, read books, research the Internet, visit museums, talk with or observe an expert, watch documentaries on television, or simply try something new.

It is important to continually increase our knowledge. The teachings we have heard for our entire lives about the importance of a good education are relevant at every age. It is critical to learn and to continue to learn, always building our knowledge base, improving ourselves. By increasing our knowledge, we will also improve our employment résumés. The needs of the world change and are now changing faster than ever before in history. If we stop learning, stop building our skills, or stop adding to our work and life experiences, we risk being left behind in the employment or business context.

The Bible tells us, *But divide your investments among many places, for you do not know what risks might lie ahead* (Ecclesiastes 11:2, NLT). Although this language may be speaking of financial investments, it is clear that our work should also be focused broadly. Ecclesiastes 11:6 (NLT) states, *Plant your seed in the morning and keep busy all afternoon, for you don't know if profit will come from one activity or another—or maybe both.* While is it often good to be an expert in an area, it is also good to have other skills, education, or experiences in case the work you are doing is replaced by a computer, rendered obsolete, or has lost its market.

Accordingly, it is important to diversify our knowledge. Just like diversifying our investments between stocks, bonds, cash, and real estate, it is good to understand and maintain transferable skills. If one investment loses value, maybe another will gain value. If one skill is no longer needed in the workplace or business world, maybe another will become of new or renewed value. Transferable skills are those that have value in one's current job, as well as for other types of jobs.

When I was a child, my mother was primarily a homemaker, and that is how she viewed her role. In addition to homemaking, she worked at times raising a few animals on our farm. She also worked in our family's small, single-butcher meat shop where we cut and wrapped meat for area farmers. My mother was in charge of wrapping the meat, answering phones, meeting the customers, and generally managing the shop. After my father died, my mother also found herself managing all aspects of the small, family-owned grocery store until she closed it when she moved to a distant community. All this time, my mother viewed herself as a homemaker. She had no formal business training. She didn't have a college degree. Yet she had significant business, managerial, and customer relations experience. All of these skills were transferable into new employment if she ever chose to pursue it. But I remember her stating one day, "But how could I get a job? I don't have any experience."

My husband and I are friends with a wonderful couple. I don't know much about the husband's formal education, but he regularly tells of a new venture such as making maple syrup, making homemade candles, or canning venison. Whenever I ask, "How did you learn how to do that?" he replies, "I wanted to try it, so I bought a book and read about it." Sometimes he says, "They had a class on that on a Saturday morning a couple years ago." He is an impressive person, as he has never stopped learning something new. He clearly enjoys learning about and experimenting with new things.

Whether we further our education formally, increase our knowledge through books and other quality sources of information, or diversify our experiences through a variety of work-life roles, the choice to continue learning is in our own hands. We can choose to watch sitcoms or reality shows on television, play video games or computerized solitaire on our laptops, or we can spend our time learning something new.

Conversely, increasing our wisdom is not something we can do as easily through books and formal education. Wisdom, like common sense, is difficult to learn in ways other than experience.

Did you ever know someone who was brilliant concerning books and tests and school, but who seemed to lack common sense? I once worked for a man I greatly respected. He knew the law and how to apply it to any given situation, but he was socially inept, obviously uncomfortable in casual settings where he was required to converse with small talk. I worked with another lawyer who could identify every conceivable legal issue relevant to the facts at hand, but she seemed unable to discern which issues were significant and which were insignificant. I have a friend who did very well in high school and college but has no sense of direction and easily gets lost.

Wisdom is not acquired through the traditional educational means.

King Solomon is known to be the wisest person of all time. The Bible tells us in the fourth chapter of 1 Kings, in verses 32 to 34, that *He spoke three thousand proverbs and his songs numbered a thousand and five. He described plant life, from the cedar of Lebanon to the hyssop that grows out of walls. He also taught about animals and birds, reptiles and fish. Men of all nations came to listen to Solomon's wisdom, sent by all the kings of the world, who had heard of his wisdom.*

King Solomon ruled over a vast territory, using his wisdom in service to God. Early on in King Solomon's reign, God appeared to him in a dream and offered to give him anything he asked for. King Solomon, recognizing that ruling the people of Israel was an enormous task, asked God for wisdom. He said, *Give me an understanding heart so that I can govern your people well and know the difference between right and wrong. For who by himself is able to govern this great people of yours?* (1 Kings 3:9 NLT). God was pleased by Solomon's request. Solomon could have asked for riches, wealth, personal happiness, a long life, or protection from his enemies; instead, he sought wisdom to be a good leader. So God not only blessed Solomon with wisdom, but he blessed Solomon with riches and honor and promised him a long life if Solomon followed his commands (1 Kings 3:10–14).

Joyful is the person who finds wisdom, the one who gains understanding. For wisdom is more profitable than silver, and her wages are better than gold. Wisdom is more precious than rubies; nothing you desire can compare with her (Proverbs 3:13–15 NLT). Those who have wisdom have joy. Wisdom is a valuable commodity, but true wisdom can neither be bought nor taught. It begins with fear of our Lord (Proverbs 9:10), as it is a treasure hidden in Christ Jesus (Colossians 2:2–3). With fear of the Lord as the foundation of wisdom, obeying God's commands enables wisdom to grow (Psalm 111:10). God gives wisdom to those who are honest and loyal to him (Proverbs 2:7–11). With generosity, God gives wisdom to those who ask for it and believe without doubt (James 1:5–6).

*For the LORD gives wisdom; and from his mouth
come knowledge and understanding.*
Proverbs 2:6

Love the Lord with all of your knowledge and your wisdom. We show that we love him by making all reasonable efforts to increase our knowledge and use such knowledge in all that we do. Using the gifts God has given us honors God. We also honor him by acting wisely, making quality decisions, and applying good judgment. Applying our knowledge and exercising good judgment in our work-lives not only benefits ourselves, but also brings value to our work, and honors God.

A Work-Life Focused on Love

A true man never frets about his place in the world, but just slides into it by the gravitation of his nature, and swings there as easily as a star.
Edwin H. Chapin,[18] American preacher, 1814–1880

Looking again at the columns rising up from the foundation of our work-life house, we see that we build our work-life choices first on a strong foundation in Christ, then we define our building blocks or columns by our passions (heart), character traits (soul), skills and abilities (strength), and knowledge and wisdom (mind). Through these building blocks, if we truly understand ourselves, we will begin to understand a piece of the work-life adventure that God has planned for us. Once we know who we are on the inside, once we know who

---

18 Chapin, Edwin H. Quote. *Quotes to Inspire.* "Confidence." 1999-2006. 04 June 2007. http://www.toinspire.com. July 2, 2012.

God made us to be, we can compare this information to the myriad of work-life opportunities and identify possibilities or possible directions. Similarly, we will be ready to quickly exclude certain employment possibilities. Knowing who we are leads us into our mission. By knowing who we are, it is much easier to identify how we are to pursue an eternal vision.

However, there is still one aspect of the greatest commandment that has not been explored. It does not suggest that we find a great job with all our heart, soul, strength, and mind. It does not state we are to earn a lot of money with all our heart, soul, strength, and mind. It does not state that we are to start our own business with all our heart, soul, strength, and mind. The greatest commandment states that we are to love the Lord our God with all our heart, soul, strength, and mind.

Loving the Lord our God is the first and foremost step in this work-life model. We start with a foundation on God, we look toward an eternal vision, and we define, develop, and use all of our heart, soul, strength, and mind to love God. Remember, love is a verb. It is not something we feel, but something that we do. In our work-lives, keep focusing on God. In time, God's purpose will shine through. In the words of Sarayu from *The Shack* by William Paul Young, *It's not the work, but the purpose that makes it special.*"[19] The purpose is to love God.

Jesus said to his disciples in Matthew 16:24–25 (NLT), *If any of you wants to be my follower, you must turn from your selfish ways, take up your cross, and follow me. If you try to hang on to your life, you will lose it. But if you give up your life for my sake, you will save it.* The key to true life, the life that God has planned for you, is to put aside all

---

[19] Wm. Paul Young, *The Shack*, Windblown Media, Newbury Park, CA, 2007, page 133.

selfish ambition and to follow Christ. Love the Lord your God. The life is in the love of God, the love of Christ. Seek life through Christ, and you will gain life beyond measure.

Reflection & Encouragement

> The supreme accomplishment is to blur the line between work and play.
> Arnold J. Toynbee,[20] British historian, 1889–1975

> Finally, the motivation for fulfilling our vocation always remains the same: to bring glory to the Creator and to serve the world out of love for Christ and for others.
> Gordon T. Smith,[21] American author and theological educator

Memory Verse

> *And whatever you do, whether in word or deed, do it all in the name of the Lord Jesus, giving thanks to God the Father through him.*
> Colossians 3:17

Closing Prayer

> Dear Father in Heaven, as my creator, you have blessed me with the desires of my heart, my passions. You have also blessed me with my special character and personality traits, my thoughts, wisdom, and education, and my special gifts, talents, and skills. Thank you. I know that I should always look to you first, as you are my first and primary passion. Forgive me when I am tempted to look to

---

20 Toynbee, Arnold. *BrainyQuote.com*. "Work Quotes." © 2001 – 2012 BrainyQuote, BookRags Media Network. July 3, 2012. http://www.brainyquote.com/quotes/topics/topic_work3.html#J130U8PWJOx8YHsL.99

21 Smith, Gordon T. *Courage and Calling: Embracing Your God-Given Potential*. Downers Grove, IL: InterVarsity Press. Copyright 1999 by Gordon T. Smith. 81.

money, prestige, or power. Bless my heart with the desire to love you and please you in all that I do. Strengthen and encourage me as I try to do what is right and good. Please show me how to apply my love for you in my work-life. Thank you, Father. Come Lord Jesus. Amen.

Make It Personal

Reading material is only somewhat useful. Applying what you have read brings the material to life. The following questions will help you to apply the main concepts of this chapter to your current work-life situation.

1. Look up the definitions for the words *success* and *significance*. Which word most likely evolves from a Spirit-based passion?

2. Think of one or more times when you were doing something and you lost all track of time. Try to come up with one example for each decade of your life. Decide specifically why you liked doing these things and make a list of them.

3. Compare the list of things you enjoy doing with the information contained in Galatians 5:16–23. Decide for yourself whether the majority of items on your list serve your sinful nature or the Spirit of God. Write a short paragraph about one thing you will try to do differently to strengthen the connection to serving the Spirit of God.

4. We gain knowledge through formal education and through work or life experiences. Make a list of special skills, knowledge, or talents you have learned through work or life experiences rather than through formal education.

5. What knowledge, skills, or talents are most often attributed to you by others? Write these down. To answer this

question, it may be useful to ask a couple close friends or family members to name three skills, talents, or other strengths that they see in you.

6. God wants you to be the person he made you to be. Take time to reflect on who you are. Write a description of your main personality and character traits. Include a sentence describing each of the following:

    a. Your social interaction style (outgoing, shy, quiet, comfortable in crowds, have many friends, few friends, talkative, or other styles);

    b. Your decision-making style (feelings or data, quick decisions or contemplative, or other factors);

    c. Your degree of spontaneity and sense of responsibility;

    d. Your sensitivity about yourself and toward the feelings of others (nurturing, matter-of-fact, blunt, or something else);

    e. Your leadership style (leader, follower, hard-driving, persuasive, etc.); and

    f. Your values (integrity, honesty, friendships, family, and more).

7. If you have access to a temperament or personality profile test, consider taking it. Although there are many good tests available, the one I like is an easy one found in the book called *Please Understand Me: Character & Temperament Types* by David Keirsey and Marilyn Bates. This book is in the list of recommended resources in Appendix B. There is also a website where one can take the *Keirsey Temperament Sorter* online and obtain a summary of the results for free. Go to http://www.keirsey.com. Alternatively, a career counseling firm or your employer may be willing to arrange a similar test.

CHAPTER 8

HERE I AM; I'LL DO IT!

Then I heard the voice of the Lord saying, "Whom shall I send? And who will go for us?" And I said, "Here am I. Send me!"
Isaiah 6:8

It's not always easy to say yes. Maybe some of you are better at it than I. When a friend or family member calls and needs a favor, is your initial, internal (perhaps unspoken) response no? Perhaps your thoughts race through a myriad of excuses: *I'm too busy. I have my own problems to resolve. I don't really know how. That's not my thing. There's nothing in it for me. That's going to cost me money and they will never repay it. I don't like doing that kind of work. Someone else can do it better than I. I'm tired. I'm too old for that. I have a bad back (at least now and then). It'll take all day. That's way too personal; I don't know them that well.*

I've had those thoughts, at least some of them, on occasion in the past. I can point to one or two of the excuses that ran through my head very recently. "Wayne, why did you sign us up to serve coffee and snacks between the worship services at church? Kitchen work is not my gift. There are other people who like this kind of thing. You should have let them sign up. And in the summer? Why would you pick summer for something like this? It is such a busy time! I just want to worship without interruption. We'll need to leave the first service early in order to be set up on time," I complained to my husband as we drove to church early on a June morning to do the volunteer job that he agreed we would do.

Excuses.

When God called me to leave my job and to work for him (just as I had requested to do through my prayers in church), I found a whole host of excuses: *I don't understand. I don't want to quit my job. What will I tell our friends? I can't afford to quit my job; we need the money. I have to work.* Some of my excuses tended to blame God for my inaction: *Your request is not logical. I don't know what you want me to do. You haven't opened new doors for me.* My excuses even tended to place my experience and knowledge above God's knowledge: *I have never recommended to anyone that they should quit their job before finding another; you can't be serious. Quitting without a plan is simply bad business; it's foolishness.* Finally, I suggested other ideas: *Maybe what you really mean is that I should find work with another employer; I'll do that.*

Excuses, accusations, and suggestions of another plan.

Making excuses is nothing new. Moses was filled with excuses when God called him to free the Israelites from Egypt. His excuses make a pretty long list: *I am nobody. I am not an influential person. The king of Egypt will not listen to me. What will I say? Who will I say sent me? They won't believe me. I don't speak well. I stammer. I couldn't possibly convince the king to free the Israelites. Just send someone else* (Exodus 3–4).

If we think excuses will free us from God's call on our lives, we are wrong. For Moses, God got angry with him. Exodus 4:14 says, *Then the LORD's anger burned against Moses.* God wasn't just a little frustrated. He didn't find Moses' excuses merely irritating. God was angry, and he was not just mildly angry with Moses. God's anger "burned" against him. That sounds frighteningly fierce to me.

At least Moses didn't claim to know more than God about the way to convince the king. Just as God's anger burned against Moses, God's anger surely must have burned against me. I had the cockiness to claim more superior knowledge than God himself, as I proceeded to make my many excuses. (*Oh, Lord, please forgive me for my arrogance.*)

As the Lord's anger likely burned against me, he continued to persuade me to say yes. During 2003, my working environment became more and more unbearable. Spewing out the specific details regarding the things that happened in my job might add color to this chapter; however, it is rarely a good idea to dwell upon such facts or to tell them to whomever you know. Instead, today, I know God was simply ensuring that I heard his call on my life. He was also strongly encouraging me to say yes.

However, the more encouragement God allowed me to receive, the harder I tried to control my own work-life destiny in my own way. For reasons that today seem illogical, I was fighting to hold on to a job I no longer wanted or enjoyed. I was fighting to hold on to a job in which my work was no longer appreciated by my boss or by my co-workers.

Working harder and harder, longer and longer hours, trying to do my job with perfection so that I would face no criticism, I found that I had less and less time with my family. I felt a huge amount of stress. I was extremely unhappy, believing that I should be able to resolve this employment situation, yet finding that nothing I did seemed to help. My family life began to suffer. My personal life began to suffer. My health began to suffer.

I recall describing my life to my sister. "I can't do it anymore," I started out dejectedly. "I can't hold on anymore. I picture the earth as a round ball with a lone leafless tree sticking up. On that tree, I hang on with all my might. The earth is turning faster and faster. It spins out of control. As it spins, the centrifugal force causes my feet to lift off the ground. The only way that I remain on earth is through the grip of my hands on the branches of the tree, my body now flying parallel to the earth's surface. I'm tired. I don't know how much longer I can hold on."

Symbolically, I look back and see that the lone tree was the cross of Christ. He was my salvation during that time and always. However, at the same time, my life was out of control. I could not continue in the situation I was in. I had a choice to make: either acquiesce to God's call or try to go it alone. His call didn't make sense to me. I didn't know how we could afford to eliminate fifty percent of our family's income and still manage our budget. I didn't want to face the embarrassment of being unemployed and looking for new employment. I didn't know that God had another plan for me. I didn't understand that God was allowing this turn of events in my work-life to encourage me to say yes to him, to encourage me to trust him.

I didn't realize it at the time, but I was in the fish's belly, just as Jonah was in the fish's belly. Jonah was called by God to go to Nineveh to tell the residents of Nineveh to change their wicked ways and follow God. Jonah knew that God had called him. He knew that God wanted him to go to Nineveh. To avoid God's call, Jonah got on a ship and began to travel in the opposite direction, headed for Tarshish. While on board the ship, the weather turned sour. There was a violent storm and the ship was struggling, about to break up. The ship and all those on board were about to be lost. Jonah finally admitted to the sailors on board that the storm was his fault. He told them that if they threw him overboard, the storm would stop. And so they did. Jonah was tossed into the sea where he was swallowed by a great fish. Jonah remained in the fish's belly until he said yes to God's call (Jonah 1–2).

I would stay in the fish's belly until I said yes to God's call. You cannot serve both God and money. *You cannot serve both God and money.* Leave your job. Quit your job and serve God. I had a choice: Face the pitfalls of my worldly choice and stay in my job, or say yes to God's call. Trust myself and my own abilities (or lack thereof) to stop my world from spinning out of control, or trust God. I reluctantly chose God. I finally said yes, even though I had no idea what God wanted me to do other than to leave my job.

I put my trust in God, and the first thing he did was to take me out of the fish's belly. The next thing he did was to tell me specifically what he was calling me to do. Write. Write a book called *My Baby's Feet*. It will have ten chapters and these are the chapter titles. Write. I'll lead as we go along. You follow.

I said yes.

It's funny how things happen. God had told me over two and a half years earlier that I was supposed to be writing and speaking. I knew it as I listened to Verla Gillmor. Yet, I didn't say yes until I was in the fish's belly.

Let's look again at Isaiah, Esther, and Moses.

Isaiah was blessed with the opportunity to say yes to the Lord. However, just before seeing the Lord, Isaiah declared out of fear that he was a man of unclean lips and that he lived among people of unclean lips. *Woe is me,* he exclaimed, certain that death would follow upon seeing the Lord. Just then, an angel came to Isaiah and touched his unclean lips with a burning coal, cleansing him of all sin, so that he would not die when he saw the Lord. After being so cleansed, when God asked, *Whom shall I send?* Isaiah could and did reply with enthusiasm, *Send me!* (Isaiah 6:1–8).

Before Isaiah was sent, he was made right with God. An angel, used of God, cleansed him of his sins. Only then could Isaiah see the Lord, hear his voice, and respond with enthusiasm.

I refer you again to Esther's story. Esther remained in the king's harem for a year, where she learned the lessons and skills she would need if she were to be selected as the wife of the king, if she ever were to become the queen. Sometime after becoming queen, Esther was called to speak to the king and save the Jewish people from destruction. Esther was trained in the king's harem for God's call long before she understood that she was being called.

Then there was Moses. He was afraid to say yes to God because he felt unqualified for the job God was calling him to do. He didn't know what he would say or how he would say it. He didn't believe that he had the speaking skills and leadership skills necessary for the job. God promised Moses that he would be with him, and Moses would lack in nothing. God would provide all necessary words, speaking abilities, and leadership abilities necessary for the job, as such skills were needed. God told Moses to simply say yes, and that he would be with Moses every step of the way.

Isaiah's relationship was made right with God before he could serve God. Esther was trained by God for her call long before she knew God was calling her. Moses needed new skills and abilities, which the Lord promised to provide when.

God works in those same ways today. He first calls us into relationship with him, making us right with him through the blood of Jesus, cleansing us of our sins. He uses our life experiences to train us for the plan he has for us. Often we may not recognize that what we are learning in one circumstance is part of God's big-picture plan for the day that he calls us into specific service for him. Finally, like Moses, if we are lacking in any manner to accomplish the work for which we have been called, God promises that he will provide. All we need to do is to step forward with a positive response to his call.

*For God is working in you, giving you the desire
and the power to do what pleases him.
Philippians 2:13 (NLT)*

I experienced this about God in my own life and in response to his call.

Although I love to read, I never thought I'd become a writer. In fact, the basic composition class in college was quite a challenge for me. Speaking in public was just as hard as writing. I intentionally took an interpersonal communications class as my speech class, so that I could avoid having to speak in front of the entire class. But apparently God had a plan for me that involved writing and speaking, and I believe that is one of the reasons I worked for so many years as an attorney.

In my first job out of college, I worked as a manufacturing engineer. It involved reading blueprints and communicating with others face to face. The most writing that I had to do was to complete pre-printed forms: check the box and fill in the blanks. This was quite different from the job requirements in my role as an intellectual property attorney. In that role, my work involved a significant amount of specialized writing for business contracts, patent applications, and licensing agreements. In all aspects of this job, writing skills were critical to success.

Writing skills were absolutely necessary. Thus, about three months after I first started working as an attorney, my boss came to my office with a brochure. "I found this class on technical writing that I thought would be good for you," he said. "Go ahead and sign up."

I signed up. I attended. It was painful. I got back to work with a sigh of relief, and life went on.

Two months later, my boss came to my office with another brochure for another writing class. *Did he forget that I already went to one?* I wondered. Not wanting to question him, I signed up. I attended. It was painful. I got back to work, again with a sigh of relief, and life went on.

Again, two months later, my boss returned to my office with yet a third writing class brochure. Fortunately for me, my boss was a patient man. By this third time I finally got the hint. *Maybe there is something wrong with my writing skills*, I thought to myself. I attended the class. I tried hard to implement the ideas and skills that I had learned.

I'll never forget the day when this same boss asked me to write a letter to someone for his signature. This occurred shortly after the third writing seminar. I knew he was testing me to determine whether I had finally learned something in the most recent seminar. The message he wanted conveyed was a simple message. I worked on it for four hours. I gave it to my boss with some trepidation, wondering to myself, *How long will he work with me on this writing issue if I don't get it right soon?* Later that day he came to my office with the letter in hand. He looked me straight in the eye and said, "This is good." Then he signed it in my presence. That was the first time my boss did not make changes to my written work. Here's the kicker: the entire letter was only one sentence long.

God's plan for me would not begin to blossom for nearly twenty years from that period of time. But first he had to teach me to write. Like Esther, he taught me necessary lessons long before he would call me to his specific plan for my life and my work-life.

Learning to write wasn't the only skill I needed to learn. Actually, the list of disciplines I needed to master was quite long. For example, I needed to learn to research an issue, study on my own, network, speak before a crowd, identify with the feelings of others, and, most importantly, always look to God. Some of these lessons he taught through my work assignments and some through specific life experiences. Some of these things were easier to learn than others, while some seemed to come naturally to me and have since become my passions. When I was younger, I would never have thought writing and research would become passions for me, but God has since placed these desires on my heart.

Learning always to look to God was a particularly difficult lesson for me. God allowed me to experience many frustrating life experiences before I learned that it was best to relinquish my life to him. Because I was so confident in my abilities, God had to humble me. He had to break my spirit so that I knew in my heart that he was in charge, and that I could do nothing without him. I was a person with unclean lips like Isaiah. I had to become right with God, which was only possible through the saving work of Jesus. It took God several years of my adult life to get me to surrender to him completely. Ultimately, I finally gave up the fight of living independently, and I looked to him through faith in Jesus.

For we are God's masterpiece. He has created us anew in Christ Jesus, so we can do the good things he planned for us long ago.
Ephesians 2:10 (NLT)

I believe that God is present in all changes if we seek him. He uses each work-life situation and its changes to prepare us intellectually, physically, emotionally, or spiritually for the next assignment that he has planned for us. Through all change, God wants us to grow.

Make a careful exploration of who you are and the work you have been given, and then sink yourself into that. Don't be impressed with yourself. Don't compare yourself with others. Each of you must take responsibility for doing the creative best you can with your own life.
Galatians 6:4–5 (MSG)

Reflection & Encouragement

All of God's people are ordinary people who have been made extraordinary by the purpose He has given them. Oswald Chambers,[22] Scottish Christian minister, 1874–1917

Moses initially had some big reservations about serving God. He ran an entire list of excuses by God. In response, God simply told Moses his name. Moses said, *I am not able to speak very well.* God replied, *I know, but I AM.* Moses worried, *I am not believable.* God remarked, *I understand, but I AM.* Moses suggested, *I am not capable.* God declared, *You're right, but I AM.* God's answer to our belief that we can't is his declaration of who he is. The answer to our worries is wrapped up in God's name. When we think, "I am not resourceful enough to serve God," just remember God's name and be reminded of his words to Moses: *I AM.*"[23]

---

[22] Chambers, Oswald. *My Utmost for His Highest*, edited by James Reimann, © 1992 by Oswald Chambers Publications Assn., Ltd., and used by permission of Discovery House Publisher, Grand Rapids, MI 49501. All rights reserved.

[23] McHenry, Raymond. *McHenry's Stories for the Soul.* Peabody, MA: Hendrickson Publishers. 2001 by Raymond McHenry, 270–271.

Memory Verse

> *Teach me to do your will, for you are my God;*
> *may your good Spirit lead me on level ground.*
> Psalm 143:10

Closing Prayer

From Hebrews 13:20–21:

May the God of peace, who through the blood of the eternal covenant brought back from the dead our Lord Jesus, that great Shepherd of the sheep, equip [me] with everything good for doing his will, and may he work in [me] what is pleasing to him, through Jesus Christ, to whom be glory for ever and ever. Amen.

Make It Personal

Reading material is only somewhat useful. Applying what you have read brings the material to life. The following questions will help you to apply the main concepts of this chapter to your current work-life situation.

1. List as many things as you can that you learned in your various work-life situations. The list may include skills, knowledge, character lessons, lessons about relationships, and more.

2. Identify a dream opportunity for serving God, something you would like to do if there was nothing in the world that could stop you. List the specific skills and talents you will need to pursue that dream. Are any of the skills and talents listed also on your list created in response to question 1 above?

3. Identify two things you can start doing now which would prepare you for the dream opportunity.

4. Responding positively to God's call might require you to take a risk, reduce your income, go back to school, or move to a new location. What steps can you take to restructure your life or finances to make a positive response to God's call easier to make? (One example might be to reduce debt by eliminating credit cards.)

5. Sometimes when facing job loss it is necessary to take a job, any job, just to stay afloat. When considering such jobs, identify what they might offer in terms of learning or networking opportunities that may be useful in the future. Try to view these interim positions from God's point of view.

   a. Try to use every opportunity you have to grow your skills, knowledge, abilities, and character. Ask yourself the following:
      i. What can I learn from this job?
      ii. How might this opportunity help me to grow intellectually or spiritually?
      iii. What positive character traits are necessary in order to do this job well?
   b. Consider how each opportunity might help you find a better position. Ask yourself:
      i. How could this job improve my résumé?
      ii. Does this job offer networking opportunities?

      iii. Will I be able to add to my list of references by working at this job?

      iv. How might this job help me to improve my work-life or my community reputation?

6. Also, when looking at such interim positions, ask yourself how you might offer a special benefit to this employer or to others you encounter on the job. For example, consider the following questions:

    a. What do I bring to this employer or job that would be of special advantage?

    b. What opportunities exist in this job for economic, quality, or process improvements that I could share with this employer?

    c. Does God want me to influence someone I encounter on this job for his kingdom?

These questions will help you to identify the diverse situations in which your skills and talents add value to the workplace. It will also help you identify opportunities for the interim employer that they may not have previously recognized. You never know when such opportunities might evolve into a more rewarding position. Finally, God might have a purpose for you in this job for this point in time, as he did with Esther.

CHAPTER 9

ACTION, ACTION, ACTION

> *"This is the first and greatest commandment. And the second is like it: 'Love your neighbor as yourself.'"*
> Jesus, Matthew 22:38–39

The heart may be willing, but the mind is still confused.

At various times in my life, my thoughts concerning my work-life direction were filled with questions, doubts, and frustration.

I am ready to say yes, but I still have no idea what I should do today or what I should do first. I still haven't seen or heard from a burning bush. I know my passions, character traits, personality traits, skills and talents, and my educational and experiential background, but I don't know what to do with that knowledge.

I'm about to lose my job and don't know what I'll do. I'm afraid I'll be demoted; how will I face everyone? I am in a work-life position that I need to change, yet there is no clear direction, no job offer, and no voice or vision directing my path. I want a *good* work-life opportunity, not just any job.

I'm ready for action, change, or opportunity, but the doors don't seem to open. I've been reading the job postings in the paper and on the Internet. I've applied to those that look interesting. Nothing happens.

New opportunities or ideas do not typically present themselves to the person who sits at home waiting for someone to knock on the door or call on the phone. Finding new opportunities requires action. Action includes networking. It is critical that we build a network, a broad circle of friends and acquaintances who provide mutual encouragement, support, information, and leads in a variety of business and personal contexts.

Network. Network. Network. I always hated the concept of networking. Every time I think about networking, my mind conjures up the salesperson who sees only themselves and their potential commission if they can convince me that I cannot live without their product. I am currently struggling with networking through social networking sites such as Facebook, LinkedIn, Shoutlife, and Plaxo. I struggle because I see many people playing a numbers game, many people simply promoting themselves or their products. I've been looking at many of these examples, trying to learn from other quality sites. I don't want to become just another social networking advertisement.

Maybe, like me, you dislike networking, but all career counselors will tell you that most jobs are found and obtained through networking. In fact, 60% to 85% of all jobs are filled through networking. The jobs are never posted to the public. The jobs are given to someone the hiring manager already knows.

It makes sense. Who would you prefer to hire, assuming each person has the basic qualifications for the job? (1) The person you have met, worked with, had the opportunity to see their enthusiasm in a professional association, or was recommended by a trusted friend? Or (2) The person about whom you know nothing, other than what he or she wrote on a résumé and what he or she claimed to be in an interview?

"But networking is so phony," you retort.

The arguments against networking may seem insurmountable to many of us. *Everyone can see right through the façade. It is obvious that they are looking for a job, even though they claim to want a meeting to gather information. They seem like hypocrites. They're just using people.*

Yes, many people understand and pursue what seems to be self-motivated networking. Some politicians are the worst offenders of self-motivated networking. They walk in parades, hand out campaign materials while shaking hands and appearing to be happy to meet everyone on the street. They don't really see anyone or bother to learn anyone's names because they are already looking ahead, searching for the next hand to shake. They don't truly notice the person who owns the hand they shake. They are too busy internally counting handshakes as votes. In truth, this type of politician is advertising; he or she is not building a network.

When I first met Wayne (my husband), I thought he was one of the worst self-motivated networkers. We met in law school. He was a senior and was the president of the Student Bar Association. I was a freshman. Every time I saw him, he had a smile on his face and appeared to be enjoying the company of those around him. *No one can possibly be that happy to see everyone*, I thought. *What a fraud.* I concluded that he was one of the worst of the worst politicians. I nicknamed him *Mr. Law School.*

In a short time, however, I discovered that all of Wayne's smiles and acts of friendliness were sincere. He was and still is a person who truly loves others. He enjoys being with and around people. His smiles and acts of kindness have consistently proven to open otherwise closed doors, break down barriers, and create opportunities. The key to his success is simply that his actions are genuine. His actions are others-motivated rather than self-motivated.

That's what real networking is all about. A network is a large group of people or organizations (such as professional associations, businesses, schools, or churches) that communicate and support each other. They help each other in areas of mutual interest. A quality network is filled with people, including oneself, who are others-motivated.

Forming or increasing the size of one's network in a sincere manner begins with the second greatest commandment: Love your neighbor. Jesus describes how such love works through the story of the Good Samaritan, the man who helped an injured man along the roadside, taking him to safety and providing for his care. Loving your neighbor involves helping him or her while expecting nothing in return. Loving your neighbor requires one to notice others, recognize their need, and step in to help to the degree they need and want help. When we love our neighbor, we look to the neighbor not to determine what the neighbor can do for us, but to determine what we can do for the neighbor.

A few years ago, my family purchased a home in the country, closing on the purchase in late fall. Initially, no one was going to live in the house, but since winter was coming, we needed help with snowplowing the driveway until more permanent arrangements could be made. So I called a neighbor. He responded with sincerity, saying that he would plow the driveway for us. I asked about payment and he replied, "I don't want to be paid. You're my neighbor. That's what neighbors do for each other." He was our Good Samaritan. He didn't worry about what he might get in return. Yet if he should ever need something, we hope to help him in return. We remain grateful for his help. That's what neighbors do.

Being a loving neighbor, co-worker, friend, acquaintance, professional, or volunteer is the biblical way to create a network. Jesus tells us in Luke 6:38, to *Give, and it will be given to you. A good measure, pressed down, shaken together and running over, will be poured into your lap. For with the measure you use, it will be measured to you.*

Give without expectation. Share your skills. Volunteer. Show that you care. Then when you have a need (whether snowplowing, a job lead, a reference, or just a hug), your need will be met. That's networking in our world today.

Love your neighbor.

From a work-life perspective, how will loving one's neighbor help us to open new doors? Loving one's neighbor will help in the work-life arena in countless ways. Allow me to highlight just a few.

Let's presume that you are currently laid off from work and you have a little spare time on your hands outside of looking for new employment. You could use the time to catch up on projects at home, or you could find ways to show love to your neighbor.

You might offer to help your neighbor with one of their projects. If you have a special skill, such as working with computers, you might offer to help neighbors, local small businesses, or local charities with possible computer issues. Trust me. If the general public is anything like me, they have computer issues and would love to get added help. Perhaps this is a time when you could hang out at a local charity, being available to do anything they might need: greeting guests, cleaning the facility, answering phones, filing, bookkeeping, or other daily tasks. Maybe you are professionally skilled. Maybe you are an attorney, human resource professional, project manager, or accountant. Many organizations would greatly appreciate help with employment policies, corporate compliance reviews and improvements, project or strategic planning support, and more, especially at no cost. Just do what you can.

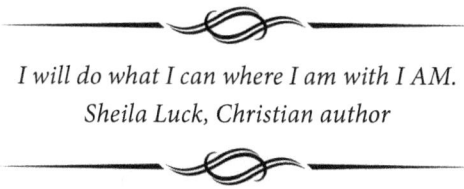

I will do what I can where I am with I AM.
Sheila Luck, Christian author

Helping our neighbors, small businesses, and local charities develops our reputation as a hard worker, increases our circle of contacts that know us, our abilities and attitude, and provides additional contacts who may be willing to give a quality job or character reference.

Perhaps it is useful to think about the following question: Do I want to be the person who is laid off and others express their pity for me? Or do I prefer being the person who is laid off and others say to one another, "I have to give him credit. He has not let this situation get him down. I am so impressed with the way he puts himself out there and gets involved. He is really a great guy"?

While loving our neighbors has an immediate, positive, earthly impact on our lives, we do not want to forget about the long-term vision for our lives. Some of us have a worldly vision for life. Some of us have an eternal vision for life. Personally, I want to hear the words *Well done, good and faithful servant* when I arrive at my heavenly home.

Jesus told the disciples about the importance of helping others. Please read the following message from Jesus, as he is speaking to his disciples.

> *When the Son of Man comes in his glory, and all the angels with him, he will sit on his glorious throne. All the nations will be gathered before him, and he will separate the people one from another as a shepherd separates the sheep from the goats. He will put the sheep on his right and the goats on his left.*
>
> *Then the King will say to those on his right, 'Come, you who are blessed by my Father; take your inheritance, the kingdom prepared for you since the creation of the world. For I was hungry and you gave me something to eat, I was thirsty and you gave me something to drink, I was a stranger and*

you invited me in, I needed clothes and you clothed me, I was sick and you looked after me, I was in prison and you came to visit me.'

Then the righteous will answer him, 'Lord, when did we see you hungry and feed you, or thirsty and give you something to drink? When did we see you a stranger and invite you in, or needing clothes and clothe you? When did we see you sick or in prison and go to visit you?'

The King will reply, 'Truly I tell you, whatever you did for one of the least of these brothers and sisters of mine, you did for me' (Matthew 25:31–40).

Those who will be judged to be righteous in Jesus' eyes are those who were kind and loving to people in need, kind and loving to the sick, and kind and loving to people in prison. Jesus says that by living lives of love toward others, caring for those less fortunate, we are showing our love for Jesus. When we love our neighbors, we show our love for Christ.

Well done, good and faithful servant. Well done.

Reflection & Encouragement

> Imagine what a harmonious world it could be if every single person, both young and old shared a little of what he is good at doing.
> Quincy Jones,[24] American musician

> We make a living by what we get, but we make a life by what we give.

---

24 Jones, Quincy. GoodQuotes.com. http://www.goodquotes.com/quote/quincy-jones/imagine-what-a-harmonious-world-it-cou. 2010. July 2, 2012.

Winston Churchill,[25] British politician, 1874–1965

Memory Verse

Each of you should use whatever gift you have received to serve others, as faithful stewards of God's grace in its various forms.

1 Peter 4:10

Closing Prayer

Father God, I come to you today, seeking your continued guidance so that I might live my life according to your will. I seek your loving discipline for my life, as I am ready, and in accordance with each of my needs. You, Lord, being all knowing and all loving, know what I need to be able to live according to your will. Please open my eyes and my heart to those around me who are needy: the weak, the hungry, the poor, and the hurting. Move my heart according to your will for my life, so that I may serve you by serving them. I pray in Jesus' name. Amen.

Make It Personal

Reading material is only somewhat useful. Applying what you have read brings the material to life. The following questions will help you to apply the main concepts of this chapter to your current work-life situation.

1. List the ways you serve(d) God by serving others in your current or most recent work-life situations.

---

25 Churchill, Winston. The Quotations Page. http://www.quotationspage.com/quote/2236.html 1994-2012 TheQuotationsPage.com and Michael Moncur. July 2, 2012.

2. Make a list of things you know how to do that might be used to help people in your community or neighborhood, local small businesses, or local charities.

3. Identify one thing you could do this week by offering to help someone in your community with one of your skills listed in response to question 2 above.

4. Pursue the item identified in question 3 above. If turned down after making an offer to help, remember to ask whether there is anything else you might help with instead. Then do it for them, assuming that you are able and have the skill. If you are not able, or if you do not have the skill, consider who you know who might be able to offer such help and make the connection.

5. Make a list of charitable causes that truly touch your heart (the list may contain only one cause or it may contain several causes). Search for and identify organizations that support your cause(s) and contact them. Ask about their volunteer opportunities and offer your help. Be sure to mention any particular technical or professional skills you can offer. Often this will lead to a more rewarding volunteer opportunity.

6. Volunteering is also an awesome way to enhance your skills in a particular field. If you need to refresh your skills or learn new ones, seek out organizations that may be willing to let you volunteer for them in exchange for the learning opportunity. This will be easiest to do through a non-profit, charitable organization, as they are accustomed to working with volunteers.

CHAPTER 10

GROWTH OPPORTUNITIES

*For God is working in you, giving you the desire
and the power to do what pleases him.*
Philippians 2:13 (NLT)

You've lost your job. You've been down-sized, right-sized, anything but super-sized. It makes you angry, embarrassed, humiliated and hurt. *I was a good employee!* you exclaim to yourself. *Why me? It's not fair!*

Management escorted you to your desk after giving you the bad news, watched you pack your personal items, and then walked you to the door, treating you like a criminal or worse. They didn't let you say good-bye to your friends. They didn't let you finish your work. They did nothing to help you preserve your dignity.

Co-workers said nothing, occasionally glancing your way. Fearful that they might be next, they kept to themselves, appearing to work hard, appearing to ignore you. Their silence made you feel abandoned.

How will I face my family, my friends, or my neighbors? I don't want anyone to know, you note to yourself as you humbly walk out with your box of personal items. *How will we make the house payment? What if our car breaks down?* Your mind races, your attitude declines and you fear the future. You are stunned, dismayed, and worried.

THE UPSIDE TO JOB LOSS

* * * * *

Your boss invited you to his office. He had a solemn look on his face. *Something's up,* you thought to yourself as you followed him down the hall to his office. *Something must be wrong.*

"Sit down," he said, pointing to a chair as he stepped behind his large and strangely clean-surfaced desk. "I have something we need to talk about." He paused, fidgeting a little. Then he added, "You are aware that the company has been looking at ways to cut costs; unfortunately, your job is going to be affected. We decided to re-organize by consolidating … blah, blah, blah … When completed, we will no longer need you in the position … blah, blah, blah … It would mean a fifteen percent cut in pay … blah, blah, blah … You'll be reporting to Kari … Sleep on it. Talk to your wife. Of course, you do understand that if you don't accept this opportunity, your decision will be considered a resignation. So, go home. Give it some thought and let me know by Friday."

Let you know by Friday? If I don't take the cut, they will declare that I have resigned? Can they do that? I'm being demoted! This is a choice? They like my work? Yeah, right. And they expect me to work for Kari? We have never gotten along. Like that will last. A cut in pay? The interest on our home mortgage just went up. Jason is starting college in the fall. Nancy's car needs to be replaced. The thoughts raced through your mind as you walked out of the office, trying to hold your head high, all while feeling like you had just been punched in the stomach.

* * * * *

I hate getting the mail, you think as you walk down your long, gravel driveway to your mailbox. *All I ever get are bills and rejection letters. Which bill should I pay this week? Which one must I pay to avoid penalties? There's just not enough money to go around. I don't know why I can't seem to find a job!* You wipe away the excess moisture building in your eyes. *I am a hard worker. I know I was a good employee. I have excellent skills! I need a job. Why can't the companies let me decide if I would be happy or not in the job? I don't care if I am over-qualified. I need a job. I'm okay with stepping down in prestige and pay. I just want to work.*

* * * * *

I hate this job. I hate working for Justin. This job is so demeaning. I have so much more to offer, but no one lets me prove it. I need to find something else. There are jobs in the city, but I'd need to move. The kids are in high school. I don't want to move them. They'd never forgive me for taking them away from their friends. But I have to do something. This job is driving me crazy. Your thoughts depress you as you slide you access card into the security lock, enter the building, walk down to the long, dingy hall to your locker. You are ready to start another seemingly endless day on the job.

* * * * *

"Business is so slow. This economy has cut my profits to nothing. I've made all the cuts I can to hang in there. I've had to lay off over fifty percent of my employees. I'm going to have trouble meeting payroll next month. I think I need to close. Do you have any ideas?" You ask your best friend and confidant. It's impossible to hide your discouragement, sadness, and sense of failure.

* * * * *

You saw it on the news. You asked you wife, "Hey! Did you see that?" You couldn't believe you heard it right. You thought the news report said the company was closing your plant. *No! I must not have heard right. They didn't say anything at work,* you think to yourself as you call one of your co-workers to see what they may have heard.

* * * * *

Our jobs are not always what we had hoped they would be. Many are not as secure as we need them to be. Some jobs just don't seem to exist. Some jobs are eliminated. Some jobs have too many applicants. Businesses fail.

Change becomes necessary.

I heard the admonition as a child. My parents said, "I don't want to do this; but it's for your own good." As painful or frustrating as it might feel, unwanted job changes are opportunities to discover God's plan for our lives. Unwanted job changes are growth opportunities. They are the beginning points for God's new work-life plans. Unwanted or unexpected job changes are new beginnings to be embraced with enthusiasm. They are a chance to discover God's new plan for our work-lives.

Transitions are times for growth in our faith and in our foundation, for growth in our vision and priorities, for growth in our hearts, our minds, our strengths, and our souls, and for growth in our ability to be others-focused.

Transition may be a time in which faith will be tested. It may be a time intended to draw one into a closer relationship with God. It may be a time of training for one's role in God's next plan. It may be God's way of telling us to do something else, to follow a new direction.

Just think of Joseph, you know, the guy in the Bible with the coat of many colors. (Joseph's story begins in Genesis 37.) Joseph was his daddy's favorite son. That's why he had such a special coat. Joseph's special treatment angered his brothers.

One day Joseph had a dream in which there were eleven bundles of grain, each of them bowing down to the twelfth bundle, the one representing Joseph. Joseph believed that the eleven bundles of grain represented his brothers, and someday they would all come to him in honor and respect, as if Joseph controlled their destiny. When Joseph told his brothers about the dream, they became extremely angry and decided to get rid of Joseph. Some wanted to kill him, but instead they sold him into slavery.

Picture his situation. One day, Joseph is living well. His life is good. He has a great coat, the best in town, kind of like owning a better house and car than everyone else. Joseph was living on top of the world. Then, with no warning, his position was eliminated, downsized, or right-sized. He was stripped of his fancy coat and led away from his co-worker-brothers, likely in shackles as a slave, no better than a common criminal.

Joseph couldn't say good-bye to his friends. He couldn't finish his work. He couldn't explain things to his father. Instead, he was escorted away. Joseph lost his job. Worse yet, Joseph lost his place in the community. He lost all of his belongings and he lost his family relationships.

I wonder what Joseph was thinking at that time. His thoughts were probably not about thanking God for this new growth opportunity. Instead, he was likely angry, embarrassed, hurt, and humiliated. He probably wondered about his future, whether he would face persecution, injury, or worse. He was likely fearful for his life. Worrying about paying the mortgage and telling his wife about losing his job might have been a welcome concern to Joseph in comparison to his actual situation.

But look at what Joseph did under these new circumstances. Without going into all of the daily details, the Bible tells us that God was with Joseph as he worked under his master Potiphar. In all ways, Joseph was successful. As a result, Potiphar put him in charge of his entire household, including the fields. Everything prospered under Joseph's care. In this position, as a slave, Joseph learned the skills of management, skills related to management of people (other household slaves) and management of materials and budgets.

But this job was not to last. Potiphar's wife falsely accused Joseph of sexually assaulting her, and Joseph was stripped of his duties and sent to prison. Joseph was fired. He was thrown into prison. He faced a new setback, another job loss, another change in status and stature. There again, God was with him, and Joseph gained favor with the prison guards. They put him in charge of the entire prison population, a much more significant role than managing the household.

While in prison, it was discovered that Joseph could correctly interpret dreams, so Pharaoh asked Joseph to interpret his dreams. Finding Joseph to be a wise man, Pharaoh released Joseph from prison and put him in charge of all the lands of Egypt saying, *'I am Pharaoh, but without your word no one will lift hand or foot in all Egypt'* (Genesis 41:44).

Famine struck Egypt and the surrounding lands, and Joseph was made governor of the storehouses of grain. Many people came to him for grain so that they would not starve. Ultimately, Joseph's brothers came to him to buy grain; however, they did not recognize him. Joseph helped them, without initially revealing his true identity.

Finally, Joseph chose to reveal his identity, saying,

> "I am your brother Joseph, the one you sold into Egypt! And now, do not be distressed and do not be angry with yourselves for selling me here, because it was to save lives that God sent me ahead of you. For two years now there has been famine

in the land, and for the next five years there will be no plowing and reaping. But God sent me ahead of you to preserve for you a remnant on earth and to save your lives by a great deliverance" (Genesis 45:4-7).

Joseph did not blame his brothers for his negative circumstances. Instead, he credited God for his positive circumstances.

Always be joyful. Never stop praying. Be thankful in all circumstances, for this is God's will for you who belong to Christ Jesus.
1 Thessalonians 5:16-18 (NLT)

Joseph made the best of his changed circumstances. He worked hard and learned as much as he could in each situation. Most importantly, at all times, Joseph remained faithful to God and God remained faithful to Joseph. Joseph's experiences as a slave and prisoner were not typical résumé-enhancing experiences, but they worked for Joseph. Each situation was a new growth opportunity designed to prepare Joseph for God's plan.

The Lord directs our steps, so why try to understand everything along the way?
Proverbs 20:24 (NLT)

Sometimes our changed circumstances are a form of discipline. Discipline too is a growth opportunity. God may want us to change our ways or follow his commands. Maybe an employer has a culture of questionable ethics, shady personal or business relationships, or illegal activity. Maybe God wants us to reject this employer and find one better suited for a walk with the Lord.

There is a story in the Bible about King Belshazzar, son of King Nebuchadnezzar, who was previously the king of Babylon. King Belshazzar was a successful and powerful king. One day he was holding a huge party for a thousand of his men. While they were enjoying their wine, drinking out of goblets taken from the temple in Jerusalem, they praised the gods of gold, silver, and bronze. Suddenly, there appeared human fingers that began writing words on the wall of the palace. No one could read the words or understand them. So King Belshazzar sent for Daniel, who was known for his knowledge, wisdom, and his ability to interpret dreams and to solve difficult problems (Daniel 5:1–17).

As Daniel read the words on the wall, he reminded the king about his father, King Nebuchadnezzar, and how God had blessed him with greatness. This is what Daniel said: *Your Majesty, the Most High God gave your father Nebuchadnezzar sovereignty and greatness and glory and splendor. Because of the high position he gave him, all the nations and peoples of every language dreaded and feared him. Those the king wanted to put to death, he put to death; those he wanted to spare, he spared; those he wanted to promote, he promoted; and those he wanted to humble, he humbled. But when his heart became arrogant and hardened with pride, he was deposed from his royal throne and stripped of his glory. He was driven away from people and given the mind of an animal; he lived with the wild donkeys and ate grass like the ox; and his body was drenched with the dew of heaven, until he acknowledged that the Most High God is sovereign over all kingdoms on earth and sets over them anyone he wishes* (Daniel 5:18–21).

God disciplined King Nebuchadnezzar because his heart had become arrogant and filled with pride. Perhaps God is using our changed circumstances as personal discipline. Perhaps a job or workplace culture conflicts with God's commands. Maybe our co-workers or managers are not walking with the Lord, drawing us into their path of sin. Discipline is a growth opportunity.

Similarly, consider the book of Haggai, chapter 1, in which God speaks to the people of Judah through the prophet Haggai. The people of Judah had become self-focused rather than God-focused. They allowed the temple of God to remain in ruins and instead worked hard to build personal wealth. Through the prophet Haggai, God said *Give careful thought to your ways. Go up into the mountains and bring down timber and build my house, so that I may take pleasure in it and be honored. ... You expected much, but see, it turned out to be little. What you brought home, I blew away. Why? ... Because of my house, which remains a ruin, while each of you is busy with your own house. Therefore, because of you the heavens have withheld their dew and the earth its crops. I called for a drought on the fields and the mountains, on the grain, the new wine, the olive oil and everything else the ground produces, on people and livestock, and on all the labor of your hands* (Haggai 1:7–11).

The people of Judah had ignored God, his temple, and their worship of him. Even though they worked hard, God did not allow their efforts to be successful. Sometimes we may feel that in spite of our strong efforts, positive results elude us. We work hard but get very little. Bonuses and promotions are handed to everyone but us.

Maybe, like the people of Judah, we have been ignoring God. Maybe we've been hoarding our earnings, our wealth, and our other gifts from God for personal use. Maybe we have not been tithing our earnings and our time. Sometimes our losses and difficulties might be a message from God to return to him, to remember always that our wealth and well-being are gifts from him, and to remember him first in gratefulness and honor and love. Perhaps this is a growth opportunity.

Therefore we do not lose heart. Though outwardly we are wasting away, yet inwardly we are being renewed day by day. For our light and momentary troubles are achieving for us an eternal glory that far outweighs them all.
2 Corinthians 4:16-17

Finally, I'd like to mention Job. Job was an extremely wealthy and blessed man. He walked closely with God. He trusted God in all circumstances. Yet God allowed Satan to destroy Job's wealth and his family, killing all of Job's children. Satan then attacked Job's health. The only thing that Satan was not allowed to do to Job was to take his life. Job's friends were certain that God was disciplining Job. They told Job to repent and to change his ways. Job knew, however, that his friends were wrong. Job lived a godly life. Job loved God and tried to live as God expected. Throughout all of this destruction, Job remained faithful to God. Even after his wife encouraged him to abandon his faith, Job remained steadfast. Job's steadfast faith, in spite of all of the horrible afflictions he faced at Satan's hand, proved his love for God, and God blessed Job. (See the book of Job for the full story.)

Consider it pure joy, my brothers and sisters, whenever you face trials of many kinds, because you know that the testing of your faith produces perseverance. Let perseverance finish its work so that you may be mature and complete, not lacking in anything.
James 1:2-4

From Job, we learn that if we remain faithful to God in all circumstances, no matter how difficult they may be, God will bless us. When our faith is being tested through seemingly unbearable circumstances, we are to remain steadfast. Our faith will be strengthened through the ordeal, and God's love will prevail. Circumstances that test our faith are also growth opportunities. Trust in the Lord in all circumstances. He will remain faithful to you, loving you and blessing you.

What growth opportunities are you currently experiencing? What are you learning? What could you be learning? Are you making the best of these circumstances? I encourage you to follow Joseph's lead, to learn all you can and to continually do your best, working at all times as though you are working for the Lord rather than for man.

Consider your way of life: Are you living a godly life? Do you try to follow God's commandments? Is the environment in which you are working one that fosters godly behavior? Remember God's discipline of King Nebuchadnezzar. Could your circumstances be a form of discipline from God?

Have you been ignoring God? Is God trying to draw you back to him, reminding you to be God-focused rather than self-focused? Are these unwanted employment circumstances the voice of Haggai for your life?

Search your heart as did Job. Pray and ask God to reveal to you just what he wants you to learn and to do. Listen for his teaching and respond positively. At all times, like Job, remain faithful. Recognize that your new circumstances create a possible growth opportunity. Remain faithful and give God praise, even when problems seem insurmountable. God has a plan for you. Focus on God and trust him. His love for you will ultimately shine through in quite possibly unimaginable ways. The sooner you understand the growth opportunity and build on it, I believe the sooner you will be able to move on, beyond the growth opportunity.

Our experiences may not be pain-free; in fact, they might be quite horrendous, but I am certain that if we remain steadfast in faith, continually drawing closer to God, we will experience his blessings in the end.

Memory Verse

> *And we know that in all things God works*
> *for the good of those who love him, who have*
> *been called according to his purpose.*
>
> Romans 8:28

Reflection & Encouragement

There is a very cute children's book about going on a bear hunt.[26] In it a family leaves home to go on a bear hunt. Throughout the story, they face many obstacles in their path, such as a scary forest, a rushing river, or deep, slushy mud. With each obstacle, they conclude that because they can't get around it, they will just have to go through it. And that's what they do.

It's a wonderful message and quite true to real life. Sometimes life throws obstacles in our paths. These obstacles include changes in our work-lives that we don't want or like. Sometimes the change seems insurmountable. We can't go under it, over it, or around it. Our only choice is to go through it. We take one step at a time. Sometimes it might feel as though we are trudging through a swamp with a mucky bottom, sinking to our knees or deeper with each and every step. We live with it, bear with it, and learn from it. As we go through it, we make the best of it. We grieve our losses and develop our new opportunities.

---

26 Rosen, Michael, and Helen Oxenbury. *We're Going on a Bear Hunt.* New York, NY: Little Simon, an imprint of Simon and Schuster Children's Publishing Division. 1989.

Follow God. Give thanks to him. God is on the path with you as you travel through periods of unwanted change.

Closing Prayer

Oh, Lord God, Father in heaven, forgive me as I lament my present circumstances. Help me to always know that you love me and you are with me during these stress-filled times. Help me to recognize and appreciate your love, and give me hope built upon the promise of your plan for my life. I need your strength and encouragement through these difficult times. Help me to remember that this is a growth opportunity. Open my eyes to the ways I might learn from this opportunity. Open my heart so I may continually draw closer to you during this time and always. Give me courage and strength to step forward in your grace. I pray these things in the glorious name of Jesus. Amen.

Make It Personal

Reading material is only somewhat useful. Applying what you have read brings the material to life. The following questions will help you to apply the main concepts of this chapter to your current work-life situation.

1. Reflect upon your circumstances and answer in writing the following questions:

    a. In what ways have I been self-centered rather than God-centered?

    b. What can I do to become more God-centered?

    c. Am I ignoring work-life opportunities that might enable me to learn a new skill?

d. Are there any educational steps I could pursue that would increase my opportunities?

2. Ask a close Christian friend, pastor, or church leader to suggest one idea that you might pursue to draw closer to God, enabling you to hear from him what he wants you to learn or do during this time. Perhaps they would be willing to help you get started on their suggestion.

3. Contact three people who work for employers for whom you might like to work. Ask them the following:

   a. Describe the type of person and type of experience that helps a person become successful with this company.

   b. Identify at least one trait that they think is most important to this employer when hiring a new employee.

   c. What additional education do they believe would be helpful for you to have when applying for a job with this employer?

   d. What additional work experience do they believe would be helpful for you to have when applying for a job with this employer?

4. Review the information gathered from question 3 above. Decide if there are any steps you could take to become more like a successful employee of your preferred employers.

Chapter 11

ONE STEP AT A TIME

*We can make our plans,
but the Lord determines our steps.*
Proverbs 16:9 (NLT)

"Be patient," my mother would say sternly whenever I would tug at her clothing as she seemed to talk endlessly with a friend. If I remember correctly, my mother could talk for hours without taking a breath. Well, maybe it wasn't really hours. She probably inhaled now and then. But as a child, I had important things to investigate. I had toys to play with, snacks to eat, and other good stuff to do. I wanted to get those things done before my mother made me take a nap. It was so hard to be patient back then.

I would grow frustrated. I wanted to get angry, maybe even throw a temper tantrum to get my way, but I knew that would only make matters worse. I tried to busy myself with something else while I waited, often getting into some form of mischief. I'd look longingly, with jealousy, at other kids leaving with their parents. I was certain that they were going to have a better day than me unless we also left for home soon. Sometimes I'd just sit and pout, giving up. I needed patience to wait on my mother's timing.

Patience.

I still struggle with the concept, even though I am over fifty years old. The lack of patience sometimes created positive results, but it usually produced negative results.

I couldn't wait to get out of high school and go on to college. I thought I had outgrown high school. There were bigger, better, and more important things to do with my life, and I believed I needed to get started right away. Luckily for me, our high school allowed us to graduate early, as long as we were enrolled in college or another form of higher education. I finished high school a semester early and started college.

Similarly, college life did not move fast enough. I chose to take more credits, go to summer school, and get it done. I thought there was a job to be had somewhere and money to be made. I didn't want to waste any time. I finished my four-year degree in three and a half years.

Initially, work and its procedures seemed so slow. Going to the same place five days each week and staying there all day long was hard for me to enjoy. It felt like prison in those early years after college. The work was okay, and the people I worked with were great. But things did not move along fast enough. It seemed that the same issue was worked, reworked, and reworked again. The days passed slowly.

Patience. I didn't have any, and in some respects my lack of patience caused me to drive forward at a faster-than-average speed in my work-life. So in some respects it was viewed positively. I preferred to get it done, now, whatever it was. I found myself often thinking or saying things like, "I'll get it done by first thing in the morning." "We can't wait that long for an answer." Or "What else can we do?"

Lacking patience can be a valuable trait in the right circumstances; however, the absence of patience has its downsides. I entirely missed the point that high school could be fun, and one might not want to leave those friends earlier than the norm. I loved college, but I was so excited about moving on to the supposedly greener pastures of the working world that I missed out on some of the extra-curricular opportunities college had to offer. I didn't live in the moment; I was always looking for the next opportunity.

My lack of patience also manifested itself in the bad habit of being late to almost everything. I didn't like waiting. I didn't like to wait for someone to arrive for lunch, or for a meeting to start, or for our daughters to come out to the car after track practice. I didn't like waiting for anything. Waiting seemed like a waste of time. I found it easier to try arriving right on time, even a little late, so I didn't have to be the one waiting.

Hey, I thought. *I have things to do. I don't have time to wait. I could get one more thing done before I leave, and then I won't have to wait when I get there. Then I will have no wasted time.* It was a good theory, but only from my personal, selfish perspective. I didn't appreciate that I was forcing everyone to wait for me.

I first began to appreciate what I was doing to others with my impatient tardiness when, as mentioned in an earlier chapter, our daughter told me why she always called when she was going to be late. She said, "You were always late when picking me up, and I would worry about you. I didn't want you to worry about me." I was quickly humbled by her words of love, and I have since tried to modify my behavior.

During the last several years, God seems to have been teaching me many lessons in patience. I mentioned earlier the time when I attended a women's retreat in Chicago and had an overwhelming, emotional response while listening to Verla Gillmor, the keynote speaker. That was the day I first heard God telling me that I too should be writing and speaking, like Verla. As I mentioned, I found myself sobbing profusely, with overpowering feelings I did not understand. I had a job. I had never thought about writing or speaking as a work-life direction. Yet I was facing this powerful and emotional grasp upon my heart.

I spoke briefly to Verla Gillmor after her speech was finished. Through uncontrollable tears, I confessed to her that she was doing with her life what God intended for me to do, but I didn't know how to get there. I asked for her advice on how to get to the life God had planned for me. She thought reflectively before answering, "God will take you there one baby step at a time. Just let him lead you and be patient. He is a lamp for your feet and a light for your path."

When I attended that retreat, I wasn't planning to write. I wasn't planning to speak to groups. I didn't even know that I might want to write or speak publicly. When I left the retreat, I returned to my overly hectic work-life as an attorney and human resources director in corporate America, and I forgot about my tears and the idea that Verla Gillmor was living my life. But God had used her to plant a seed. It was eight months later when I prayed, asking God to let me be his employee.

God has his own plan and his own timetable. Sometimes we need to be patient. Just like what Verla Gillmor told me, God will bring you along one step at a time. *[God's] word is a lamp for my feet, a light on my path* (Psalm 119:105).

About eighteen months after asking God to hire me, I left my job with corporate America and wrote my first word, leading to my first manuscript entitled *My Baby's Feet*. Writing that book was an experience of extreme personal reflection. God took me one step at a time through an earlier point in my life, a time that I had tried to forget for years. I appreciated the walk, and I understood why the walk was necessary, but I wanted it to end at the same time.

"Aren't we done yet, God? Haven't I worked on this long enough? What is it that you want from me? Why are you not helping this move forward? I can't stand the solitude. I can't stand the waiting. I need more!" I prayed fervently and angrily and with a sense of impatient desperation. His answer, over and over and over seemed to be, "Wait. I'm not finished with you yet. I'll let things move forward when you are ready." "But I'm ready now!" I'd argue with him in my prayers.

I wanted action. I wanted progress. Frustration would arise out of my impatience. I'd observe with a twinge of envy other speakers, wondering why it seemed that God had called me to this role but not opened any doors. I frequently doubted God and his plan for me. I often wanted to retreat back to the corporate world working as an attorney. It was an employment direction that I understood, a world that was familiar to me. I wanted to give up on God's call on my life. He wasn't making it easy. Frustration, envy, doubt, and a desire to give up – these feelings were not unlike those felt as a young child as I waited for my mother. Now I felt them as I waited on the Lord, waited for his timing and for his plan for my life to continue to unfold.

Wait for the Lord; be strong and take heart and wait for the Lord.
Psalm 27:14

Patience.

I wanted to speak about the topic of *My Baby's Feet* to youth groups, women's groups, and churches. Of course, I now remembered Verla and the emotional discovery that I was called to write and to speak. When the first opportunity arose, I accepted it excitedly. I could do this. This was my big break. After accepting the opportunity and following through with it, I knew in my heart that I had forged ahead on my own and not according to God's plan. I tried to force something that was not ripe, just like eating fruit that hasn't ripened. It may be hard, potentially bitter. I had been impatient.

From that point on, I knew I needed to wait patiently before taking each step forward. My hard driving type-A personality had to learn to wait for God's timing and for God's lessons for me. Only when I was ready in his eyes would he allow me to take the next step forward.

There are a number of reasons why God might make us wait before he opens the next door. In my case, I had a lot to learn. I needed intellectual, emotional, and spiritual growth. God was a light for my path. In my personal situation, God wanted to mold me, ensure that I was truly ready for the work he had planned for me. He knew I was not ready for that first speaking engagement. God knew. I did not. Rushing things rather than waiting on God was a mistake for me.

In Jeremiah 18:1–6, God showed Jeremiah just how he prepares us for his service. God prepares us in a manner similar to that used by a potter creating a pot. If the pot isn't what it needs to be, the potter re-shapes it. He works with it again and again, as may be needed, until it is right in his eyes. We need patience while God works with us.

Being patient while God works with us, molding us and shaping us, is contrary to how most of us have been taught for much of our lives. Career counselors, supervisors, mentors, and American society in general often discourage waiting. Instead, we are told in many different ways that we need to get out there and pursue all that we can be and all that we can get, as quickly as possible. Life is short. If we want to make something of ourselves, we are often taught to get moving now.

To the contrary, maybe we are not ready to go to college. My husband worked in construction for three years between high school and college. Maybe it is best to accept the introductory position rather than the supervisory position. Perhaps there is merit in working one's way up to the job, gaining greater responsibility to ensure competence. Is six months or one year long enough in a job to be fully proficient at the job? It depends on the type of work. Some professional positions take years to master. Maybe doors are not opening because experience is lacking.

Abraham and Sarah chose to rush things by taking matters into their own hands rather than waiting on God. God had promised Abraham that he would have many descendants, yet as the years passed, his wife Sarah never became pregnant. Ultimately, Sarah stopped waiting on the Lord, doubting that he was going to follow through as promised and believing that she had a better plan for starting their family. Instead of waiting on the Lord, Sarah gave her maidservant Hagar to her husband, believing that they could build a family through her. Hagar conceived and gave birth to a boy. Unfortunately, the pregnancy and birth were not reasons for joy for Sarah. While pregnant, Hagar began to despise Sarah and treated her very badly. Sarah blamed Abraham for all of the trouble with Hagar and demanded that he do something about her. Abraham told Sarah that she could treat Hagar as she pleased, so Sarah treated her so badly that Hagar fled from their home, taking her son with her (Genesis 16:1-6).

Sarah's impatience created strife between her and her husband. As a result, the maidservant and her son were forced to leave their home. Clearly this was not God's intent when he promised Abraham and Sarah a child. This difficult situation was created when Sarah, lacking patience, pushed her own agenda. She doubted God's promise and direction and failed to wait for God's timing.

Sarah ultimately became pregnant, but not until she was more than ninety years old. Who would have guessed that? God lives with a vastly different timetable than our own. Trust him and wait on him, even when his response seems unlikely and perhaps even impossible.

God is never early; God is never late. Trust his timing. Do not cater to feelings of doubt. Feelings of doubt often result in stepping forward without God and apart from his divinely planned time.

As in my case, patience is often a necessary part of our growth opportunities. Yet there may be other reasons for which God's answer to us is to wait, reasons that are not directly related to our personal circumstances. There are other people in this world and in God's kingdom, and in God's eyes the entire picture must unfold in accordance with his plan. For example, one's next opportunity might be in another location, but it may not be the right time to move one's family. Maybe God's plan is for us to work with or near another person, but the particular job has not yet opened.

It is sometimes hard to imagine the many reasons why God needs us to wait patiently, because we cannot see our lives and our world from God's perspective. A speaker once suggested that our lives are like a single thread in a tapestry. There are numerous other threads, colors, and woven images on the face of the tapestry. Sometimes we have a visible role in the picture of the tapestry. Other times, we are in the background, traversing the tapestry on our own road of life, but not necessarily visible. These are the moments in which patience is required.

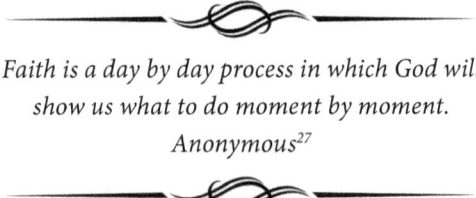

Faith is a day by day process in which God will show us what to do moment by moment.
Anonymous[27]

Waiting on the Lord doesn't necessarily mean that we do nothing until he guides us to the next open door. It doesn't mean that we sit

---

[27] McHenry, Raymond. *McHenry's Stories for the Soul*. Peabody, MA: Hendrickson Publishers. 2001 by Raymond McHenry. 103.

and pout as I did when waiting for my mother as a child. It doesn't mean that we just hang around home watching television, expecting the next opportunity to show up in an email or on Facebook, LinkedIn, or another networking site over the Internet. Instead, we should prayerfully take steps forward, not so much that we are pushing our own agendas, but rather in a manner that we are testing the waters, pressing against the various doors to see which will open. As we test the waters or press against the various doors, it is most important that we remain close to God, keeping our ears, eyes, and heart open to his ultimate call. An excellent example of this can be observed in this story about Paul as told in Acts 16:6–10.

Paul and his companions traveled throughout the region of Phrygia and Galatia, <u>having been kept by the Holy Spirit</u> from preaching the word in the province of Asia. When they came to the border of Mysia, they tried to enter Bithynia, <u>but the Spirit of Jesus would not allow them to.</u> So they passed by Mysia and went down to Troas. <u>During the night Paul had a vision</u> of a man of Macedonia standing and begging him, "Come over to Macedonia and help us." After Paul <u>had seen the vision, we got ready at once</u> to leave for Macedonia, concluding that God had called us to preach the gospel to them. [Emphasis added.]

When Paul tried to preach in Asia and in the province Bithynia, the Holy Spirit prevented him from preaching. Even though these doors were not opened to Paul, he did not give up. He continued on to the next location. Eventually, God gave Paul specific direction through a dream or vision, and Paul wasted no time in responding.

Paul pressed forward, but at all times remained open to the promptings of the Holy Spirit. His story shows us that it is good to step forward, as long as we remain in the Lord, listening and responding to his direction. Paul's story also makes it clear that we are not to give up when doors are closed. Continue pursuing the next opportunity and the next, until a door opens or until God's direction becomes clear. At some point, you will sense when you are on the right path, maybe through a vision, maybe through a dream, or maybe simply from the recommendation of a trusted friend.

Wait patiently and don't give up. While waiting, consider whether this period is a growth opportunity. Learn from it. Draw closer to God and know that he has a plan for you. In his time, he will open the door that is right for you. Let God be your hope in your upside-down world.

But as for me, I watch in hope for the Lord, I wait for God my Savior; my God will hear me.
Micah 7:7

Reflection & Encouragement

Waiting isn't about what happens outside you—it's about what happens inside you.

Always, always, when you wait, no matter what you *think* you're waiting for, you—and God—are always waiting on changes and discoveries inside yourself. God needs those changes and discoveries before you can do the next job He has for you. He has a plan, a blessed syllabus for your life, and it's always charted from the inside out.

When your wait is over, the outward one that you can see, it's because you've accomplished the work that God had for you to do inside yourself *during that wait*, and you and He together will know when that happens.

Karen Phillips Goodman[28]

---

[28] From *You're Late Again, Lord!*, published by Barbour Publishing, Inc., Uhrichsville, OH. Used by permission.

Memory Verse

> *There is a time for everything, and a season for every activity under the heavens.*
>
> Ecclesiastes 3:1

Closing Prayer

Father God, I thank you for molding me, as with clay, as I face change in my life and in my work-life. I also thank you for molding me during periods of waiting. Help me to see your hand in each step and in each delay. Enable me to learn what you want me to learn so that I may serve you to the fullest extent possible in your ultimate plan for my life. As I wait for your perfect timing, I sometimes grow impatient and try to take matters into my own hands. Please forgive me for my impatience. In the words of David, from Psalm 25:4–5, I ask that you *show me your ways, Lord, teach me your paths. Guide me in your truth and teach me, for you are God my Savior, and my hope is in you all day long.* Amen. Come Lord Jesus.

Make It Personal

Reading material is only somewhat useful. Applying what you have read brings the material to life. The following questions will help you to apply the main concepts of this chapter to your current work-life situation.

1. List three ways how God might tell us no or not yet, when we are pursuing a new job or employment direction.

2. List three ways that God might tell us it is time to move in a new direction.

3. Describe a time when you had to wait patiently. In hindsight, what do you think you learned from that experience?

4. Describe a time in your life when you pursued a new work-life opportunity, but it did not pan out. Try to view this situation from God's point of view and list three possible reasons why he did not open that particular door for you.

5. God may use times of waiting to help a person grow educationally, spiritually, relationally, or emotionally. Come up with at least one thing you could do during a period of waiting that might help you grow as a person in each of the above categories.

WORDS OF CLOSURE

We live in an ever-changing world. We face changes in life that might make us feel angry or rejected or anxious. We know that God has a purpose for us, and he gave us talents, skills, and passions to use in service to him, according to his will. We understand that we may need to be patient, as we may have something to learn first. Now it is time to look forward. Begin moving forward with an eternal destination in mind.

Sometimes we may not understand God's plan for our lives for many years. Remember, God will mold us just as a potter molds his clay. As the process continues, we will be able to define a mission for our lives. As time passes, God may move us onto another path, and our missions may evolve. Regardless of the changes, however, it is important to keep focused on God, on Christ Jesus, and on his kingdom. With a vision focused on his kingdom, our individual missions will become clearer.

When we draw near to the Lord, he will draw near to us. He will direct our paths. As we listen to his call, seek his direction for our personal lives and our work-lives, new doors will open, opportunities that bring the desires of our hearts, often in ways we never imagined. When facing adversity, remember that it is a growth opportunity. God prepares us for his plan for our lives. When we each hear him call, asking who he shall send, I pray that we each step up enthusiastically with a resounding, "Yes! Here I am. Send me."

I leave you with the following words of the apostle Paul, written originally to the church at Thessalonica, and ultimately to all believers everywhere, including you.

And we urge you, brethren, to recognize those who labor among you, and are over you in the Lord and admonish you, and to esteem them very highly in love for their work's sake. Be at peace among yourselves.

Now we exhort you, brethren, warn those who are unruly, comfort the fainthearted, uphold the weak, be patient with all. See that no one renders evil for evil to anyone, but always pursue what is good both for yourselves and for all (1 Thessalonians 5:12–15 NKJV).

> *May God be with you today and always.*
> *In his love, Sheila M. Luck*

APPENDIX A

Using This Book as a Small Group Resource

This Appendix A has been added to aid in the use of this book as a small group resource.

There are eleven chapters plus an introduction to this book. Therefore, group facilitators are encouraged to schedule twelve meetings to complete this book study, using the first meeting to do the following:

1. Get to know each other. Request that each person introduce themselves and state why they chose to participate in this group and book study.

2. Discuss the schedule and any other relevant logistics (snacks, time, holidays, and handling of last-minute cancellations due to weather or other emergencies).

3. Encourage each participant to read each chapter and answer the questions contained in the "Make It Personal" section of each chapter before attending the small group. However, schedules are tight, and participants should be encouraged to attend the group meetings, even if they did not complete the particular chapter beforehand.

4. Develop trust within the group. (Further discussed below.)

5. Review the introduction to the book.

6. Ask if the group would like to share email, phone, or other contact information. Handle accordingly.

Each weekly session will require approximately ninety minutes to complete, depending on the number of participants and their degree of comfort in participating in a group book study. Good meetings start on time and end on time. Attendees often have other obligations, whether with family or jobs or appointments. Please be respectful of the participants' time.

Active participation may lengthen the time spent in discussion, thereby inhibiting timely completion of all discussion questions listed for each chapter. Please do not view this as a problem, as each participant can be encouraged to complete any remaining questions independently. Active, applicable discussion is often the most valuable portion of any small group book study. Allowing participants the freedom to discuss questions or issues most pressing on their hearts is often more valuable than focusing on the discussion questions that I, as the author, proposed. Sometimes the group may want to skip a question or discuss the questions in a different order. Feel free to manage the discussion in whatever way works best to encourage active discussion. On the other hand, except in the case of an urgent need for personal support, the group facilitator is strongly encouraged to guide discussions so they remain generally on topic.

Active participation requires trust among one another. Trust, however, can often take weeks, months, or years to develop in average social contexts. To shorten this process, please discuss the importance of respecting each group participant by listening, sharing, and responding in love; and obtain agreement by the group participants that they will maintain all personal comments and disclosures as confidential. To this end, the following language may be read aloud to the group if desired:

This group is intended for men and women of all ages. It is for those who may be wondering what God's plan is for their lives and in their world of work, whether their work is paid employment, home and family service, volunteer work, or education. Figuring out God's plan for our lives is exciting, rewarding, and sometimes a little – or even a lot – uncomfortable. The purpose of this group is:

- To share the love, grace, and mercy of Jesus Christ with each other by sharing and bearing each other's burdens and joys, expressing our love and care for one another, and encouraging each other.

- Some people are very comfortable sharing their thoughts, feelings, concerns, worries, or fears within a group context. Somehow they naturally feel a sense of love, trust, and freedom. But for many of us, it takes a while to build that feeling of confidence and trust with the others in the group.

- Trust is needed before true sharing is possible. Trust is based on the knowledge that all group participants will respect one another, will be honest, will keep confidences, and will not gossip or criticize. Be aware that body language and facial expressions often speak louder than words. Trust is based on the knowledge that all group participants will treat each other with love, encouragement, and care. Accordingly, please promise to act as loving, trustworthy friends, and brothers and sisters in Christ in all that you say and do in this group.

- To encourage the development of trust, a promise of love and confidentiality is requested of each participant. Please state whether you are willing to make such a promise.

Thank you for enhancing each other's experience with this book through your participation in a book study. More importantly, thank you for supporting one another as you travel down this path of work-life change together. I pray that you enjoy and learn from this book by developing a closer relationship with our Lord Jesus Christ. I encourage you to keep in contact with each other when this group study is completed, helping each other discover God's plan for your work-lives.

Meeting 1: Introduction

Opening Prayer

Father God, we are so grateful you are God, King of kings, God of gods, Master of all things. We are thankful that we do not have to be in control, because sometimes our personal lives seem to spin out of control. At this time, many of us are facing work-life changes, job loss, or other employment rejection. These changes may cause us to feel disappointment, discouragement, a sense of failure, sadness, anger, worry, or embarrassment. We come to you today, and every day, knowing that you have a plan for our lives. We seek your guidance and your loving, supportive, encouraging touch. Please be with our group as we try to draw closer to you through this book study. Enable us to hear your voice and open our hearts to your call, so that we can each discover and pursue the plan that you intend for our work-lives. Thank you, dear Father. We pray in Jesus' name. Amen.

Discussion

1. Introduce yourselves and state why you chose to participate in this group and book study.

2. Discuss the schedule and any other relevant logistics (snacks, time, holidays, and handling of last-minute cancellations due to weather or other emergencies).

3. Each participant is requested to read each chapter and to answer the questions contained in the "Make It Personal" section of each chapter before attending the small group. However, because schedules often get away on us, you are encouraged to attend the group even though you may not have completed a particular chapter before our meeting.

4. Trust within the group enhances active participation. A volunteer is asked to read aloud the segment on trust written in italics in the beginning of this Appendix A.

5. Look through the introduction to the book. Discuss anything that specifically caught your eye, confused you, or encouraged you.

6. Decide among group participants as to whether you would be willing to share email, phone, or other contact information. The facilitator is encouraged to circulate a sheet of paper for this purpose, make copies, and distribute them at the next meeting of the group or through email.

7. Are any group participants on Facebook? The author has formed a Facebook group entitled "The Upside To Job Loss." This is a public group. All participants are invited to join the group where you can further discuss the book, pose questions to the author, and network with others. Go to www.facebook.com/sheilamluck to find the author's page and access to the group.

Meeting 2: Chapter 1 – Go Boldly!

Opening Prayer

Dear heavenly Father, Creator of all things, we are so thankful for this opportunity to begin studying your Word as it relates to our work-lives. Sometimes we find ourselves in the middle of a change, wondering, "What should I do now?" Sometimes we hear your call on our lives, and sometimes you seem to be silent. We pray that through the next several weeks you will be with us, you will guide our conversations, and you will help us to identify your will as it relates to our lives. Bless us today, dear Lord. We pray in Jesus' name. Amen.

Discussion

1. Please tell the group your name and one answer you gave as a child when asked, "What do you want to be when you grow up?"

2. List the fears and concerns that people may face today when leaving a known work-life situation, whether voluntarily or involuntarily, for a new or unknown work-life situation.

3. Work-life changes may involve grieving over anticipated, perceived, or actual losses. Stages of the grieving process include denial, anger, bargaining (attempts to prevent the change by offering alternate solutions), depression, and acceptance. Are any of these stages evident in the story about Henry and his job loss? Please explain.

4. If we focus primarily on the difficulties of work-life change or on our fears regarding such change, instead

of on Jesus and God's plan for our lives, what might be the result?

5. What can we do to help keep our focus on Jesus?

6. Imagine that you are in a work-life situation involving something that is morally, ethically, or legally wrong. Discuss the likely risks and rewards of doing what is right in such a situation. (It may help to read about Moses to answer this question. See Exodus 2:11–25.)

Meeting 3: Chapter 2 – Why Me? Why Now?

Opening Prayer

Dear Lord, God of the heavens and earth, thank you for again giving us this opportunity to study your Word as it relates to our work-lives. Some of us are facing a pending change in our work-lives, and others of us are in the middle of the change. In either case, we may be feeling disappointment, anger, or hurt, as we try to figure out what to do next. Bless us through your Holy Spirit with the grace needed to forgive all those who may have angered or disappointed us, placing us in these situations of unwanted change. We pray, Lord Jesus, come. Come to us and support us as we struggle with these changes. Open our eyes to your will and provide to us healing for our hearts, so we may move forward according to your plan. Amen.

Discussion

1. Please describe a time in your life when you were facing something new but not looking forward to it. How did it turn out?

2. When one faces an unwanted work-life change, there are many actual as well as perceived losses. Identify at least five losses people may face or experience as their work-life changes.

3. Now that you've discussed losses, discuss the positive aspects one might discover as a result of an unwanted work-life change. Please try to identify at least five positive aspects of work-life change.

4. When facing an unwanted work-life change, a person might be angry with his or her boss, co-workers, potential employers, spouse, self, or God. Discuss why, in the context of each person or relationship.

5. It is important to maintain positive relationships with the people in our past and present work-life situations, even though we may currently feel anger or disappointment. Discuss why.

6. Discuss ways to dispel our anger that are most likely to maintain or create positive relationships with those with whom we are upset.

7. Colossians 3:15 says, *Let the peace of Christ rule in your hearts, since as members of one body you were called to peace. And be thankful.* Discuss how forgiving others will impact our hearts and why.

Meeting 4: Chapter 3 – Worry, Worry, Worry

Opening Prayer

Dear Father, we thank you for your love and faithfulness, which gives us the strength to get through difficult times of change, times that often create feelings of frustration and anger. In addition to these feelings, some of us worry during times of change, particularly if we were not as prepared for the change as we could have been. If we have been lax in our responsibilities to ourselves, our families, or to you, O Lord, please forgive us. Even when we are prepared for a work-life change, some of us still worry. We ask that you come to us today as we study your Word. Bless us with your peace and hope, and strengthen our faith in you, so we may put our feelings of anxiety away. Thank you, dear Father. Amen.

Discussion

1. Share with the group something you did when you were young and perhaps believed you were invincible. Would you do that today if given the opportunity? Why or why not?

2. Discuss aspects of our work-lives that we might commonly worry about (financial worries, for example), and describe how such worries might impact our work-life choices.

3. Discuss what steps one could take to create a *safety net*, which would make it easier to consider, pursue, or deal with a sudden work-life change.

4. Jesus told the disciples that life is more than food and clothing. Identify elements in life that are more important than food and clothing. To help make this list, try to consider the list from God's point of view.

5. Jesus said that we should seek his kingdom. How will seeking his kingdom help us when there is an unwanted

work-life change? What actions can we take to seek his kingdom?

6. Discuss what Jesus may have meant when he said that we should *Provide purses for yourselves that will not wear out, a treasure in heaven that will never fail, where no thief comes near and no moth destroys* (Luke 12:33).

Meeting 5: Chapter 4 – Rejected Again

Opening Prayer

Abba, our Father, the One who is love, we thank you for the love you pour upon us. We are honored, yet unworthy, to be called your children, positions that cannot be earned. We are so grateful. Sometimes in our work-lives we face hurtful rejection, and it wears us down. We long to find meaningful work-life opportunities. Sometimes doors remain closed to us, and then we face harmful feelings of rejection. Please help us to know you and maintain a strong foundation in your love and all other things necessary to remain confident in spite of rejection. In Jesus' name we pray. Amen.

Discussion

1. Please describe something you've done that felt like a particularly special accomplishment, something that enabled you to feel proud of yourself.

2. It is common for people to ask a new acquaintance, "What do you do?" Some people incorrectly feel that the answer defines who they are and their social status. Instead of saying what you do, tell the group who you are.

3. Repeated rejection is often demoralizing. Discuss what a person might do to keep their spirits up when facing rejection or a sense of failure.

4. Many of us have faced a jealous co-worker, boss, or friend. Describe how jealousy might arise in a work-life situation today in the form of rejection or a similar negative behavior.

5. How should we respond in our work-lives when dealing with jealousy, rejection, or poor behavior by others? For ideas, see Psalm 37:1–6.

6. Romans 5:3–5 states, *Not only so, but we also glory in our sufferings, because we know that suffering produces perseverance; perseverance, character; and character, hope. And hope does not put us to shame, because God's love has been poured out into our hearts through the Holy Spirit, who has been given to us.* Discuss how suffering rejection might produce hope in the work-life context.

Meeting 6: Chapter 5 – Your Destination

Opening Prayer

Father, God, Creator of all things, we know you have created us for your purposes and that you have placed us on earth for only a short time. Forgive us when we do not spend our time in ways that honor you and serve you. Help us to maintain our focus on you rather than on worldly, selfish desires. Be with us today as we study your Word. Show us how we might live and act according to your will, as mem-

bers of your holy family, and always in your honor. In Jesus' name we pray. Amen.

Discussion

1. Describe one trait you might like others to remember about you after you have died.

2. It is common for corporations to set the vision for their employees through a vision statement. That statement is intended to define the company's ultimate destination. From God's perspective, what is the *end*, when we are talking about our ultimate destination?

3. Jesus said, *Enter through the narrow gate. For wide is the gate and broad is the road that leads to destruction, and many enter through it. But small is the gate and narrow the road that leads to life, and only a few find it* (Matthew 7:13–14). Name a common career goal and describe whether such a goal might be part of the *wide* gate or the *narrow* gate? Why?

4. As part of her eternal vision, the author hopes to hear the words, "Well done good and faithful servant," when she meets Jesus in heaven one day. Brainstorm a list of elements that might be part of an eternal vision for one's life.

5. Discuss ways an eternal vision might impact one's work-life choices.

6. Discuss the difference between vision and mission.

7. When identifying your mission, it is useful to understand elements of your own story. Make a list of ten such ele-

ments. Examples include family circumstances or your community.

Meeting 7: Chapter 6 – God Called

Opening Prayer

Dear Lord, Father of us all, you are our Creator and Redeemer. Be with us today as we study your Word about your purpose for our lives. We want to understand what you want to accomplish through us now and in the future. We want to hear you with open ears and open hearts when you speak our names. We want to respond to your voice willingly. Enable us to hear you, Lord. Grant us the ability to discern your voice from all other calls upon our lives. We pray in Jesus' name. Amen.

Discussion

1. Discuss ways that God might use to encourage a person to move toward the purpose he intends for him or her.

2. What can a person do to discern whether his or her feelings or changing circumstances are actually a call from God?

3. Jesus said, *I am the good shepherd; I know my own sheep, and they know me, just as my Father knows me and I know the Father* (John 10:14 NLT). Based on Jesus' words, if we know him, we will recognize his voice and follow him. What can we do to know Jesus?

4. Oswald Chambers states that sometimes we don't hear God's voice because we are too devoted to things, to

service, or even to our own convictions. What do you think he meant?

5. Esther's story reflects the truth of Psalm 37:3, which says, *Trust in the Lord and do good, then you will live safely in the land and prosper* (NLT). Discuss what happened in the story of Esther that reflects the truth of this verse.

6. God sometimes calls us to do things that do not fit with our plans, like Esther. What lessons can we learn from Esther that can be applied to our work-lives?

Meeting 8: Chapter 7 – When in Doubt, Start with His Command

Opening Prayer

Dear Lord, our Father in heaven, your faithful love never ends. Again we thank you, dear Father, for bringing us together to grow in our understanding of your plan for our work-lives. We pray that you continue to guide us as we study your Word. Be with us as we think about our favorite activities, hobbies, and service opportunities. Help us to recognize our hearts' desires and passions affiliated with these things. Clarify for each of us the special character and personality traits, physical abilities, talents, and special gifts with which we have been blessed. Grant us wisdom for the moment and wisdom for our lifetimes, so that we make loving, wise choices in honor of you. Help us to show our love and honor for you in all we do and all that we pursue. Amen.

Discussion

1. Please describe a favorite hobby and explain what you like most about it. Identify one skill needed in this hobby that might also be useful in a job.

2. How does pursuing one's passion in their work-life model loving God with all of your heart?

3. Identify five character or personality traits and list a few jobs for which each character trait or personality trait would be of a particular benefit. For example, being outgoing is a good personality trait for sales jobs.

4. Someone once said that one can learn the techniques of art and design in school, but the education will never give a person an eye for it. What do you think this means? What other skills or talents are God-given gifts that cannot be fully learned through education and training?

5. Should one concentrate most on improving their weaknesses or building upon their strengths? Why?

6. Discuss why using our passions, character traits, strengths, education, experience, and wisdom in our work-lives shows love to God.

Meeting 9: Chapter 8 – Here I Am; I'll Do It!

Opening Prayer

Almighty God, Lord of all, you can do all things without limitation. Still, you invite us to serve you in a variety of ways. We thank you for giving us the talents we need and teaching us how to use our talents with love, compassion, and in honor of you. Help us to learn all that you want us to learn through each of our work-life experiences and the changes we often face. Today we ask that you strengthen our faith through the study of your Word, giving us the confidence we need to serve you, trusting that you will provide all skills and abilities needed as we seek to do your will. Amen.

Discussion

1. Imagine the stereotypical reactions of a dog and of a cat when its owner calls its name. If you believe that Jesus is calling, do you think you will be more like a dog or a cat when you answer? Explain.

2. Over twenty years had passed from the time the author graduated from college to the time she began writing and speaking in service to God. As the author now looks back, she is able to draw a tie between the work-life experiences and her current service to God. What does this say about the likelihood that we will fully understand God's plan for us during each work-life situation or change?

3. Do we need to fully understand God's plan for us in order to learn from our circumstances? Why or why not?

4. God did not open new doors for the author until she gave up her security blankets such as her current job and her paycheck. Why do you think God waited until then before guiding her next steps?

5. Share something you had to learn, or a skill that needed to improve, which enabled you to take the next step in accordance with God's plan for your work-life.

6. How do we know that we will have the necessary skills when God calls us for a purpose?

7. Name one skill you have mastered now that will prepare you for an anticipated or desired future opportunity.

Meeting 10: Chapter 9 – Action, Action, Action

Opening Prayer

Dear Father in heaven, thank you for this time together with friends. We so often get caught up in our own problems, concerns, or just plain busyness that we fail to notice your many blessings. We also fail to notice others in need and how we might help them. Please forgive us for being self-focused. Please bless our conversations today, such that our hearts may be opened to others. Help us to be others-focused, noticing their needs, recognizing our opportunities to help, and acting upon those opportunities. Help us to continually live out your love with others, doing what we can, where we are, with you. We pray in Jesus' holy name. Amen.

Discussion

1. The saying goes, *It is better to give than to receive.* Why would this be true?

2. Do you agree with the following statement? Helping others blesses me more than it blesses those I help. Why or why not?

3. Discuss ways to recognize or identify the needs of those around you.

4. If a person has not asked for help, should you still offer help? What should you do if they turn you down? Share with each other example situations.

5. The second greatest commandment is to love our neighbors. Who are your neighbors in the context of your work-lives?

6. What can you do to make the work-lives of others around you better (i.e., your boss, coworkers, employees, customers, or clients)?

7. How might helping others help you in your work-life?

Meeting 11: Chapter 10 – Growth Opportunities

Opening Prayer

Dear Father in heaven, we love you. Forgive us if we have failed to express this love in all that we are and in all that we do. Thank you for this group with whom we can share our disappointing circumstances, our thoughts, and our concerns. Many of us do not want our work-lives to change. We worry about our families, our finances, and our futures. Please help us to grieve our losses and to manage these changes as opportunities to grow in faith, to learn your will for our lives, and to persevere with renewed strength. Help us to recognize the areas of growth that you see for our lives, whether it is growth in our foundations, in our visions, in our hearts, in our souls, in our minds, in our strengths, or in our love for others. Thank you for these growth opportunities. Thank you for continually working with us, for not giving up on us, and for preparing us for the ultimate plan you have for our lives. Amen.

Discussion

1. Share with the group an example of a person who faced an unwanted work-life change but is now happy with their new work-life situation.

2. Brainstorm reasons why God might allow an unwanted work-life change to happen in our lives. Try to list at least ten reasons.

3. Share with the group at least one way in which you have grown, either during this time of work-life change, or during such a time in your past.

4. As a group, try to identify ten things a person could do to identify the growth and/or learning opportunities in an unwanted work-life change.

5. Identify one of the items on the list of ten (from question 4 above) that you are willing to try tomorrow. Share with the group why you selected this item and what, if anything, you hope to discover when you try.

Meeting 12: Chapter 11 – One Step at a Time

Opening Prayer

Heavenly Father, as we keep our sights on you, we often find your call and will for our lives overwhelming. We may need more education, more experience, or more talent. We pray that you provide these things for us when we need them and as we are ready. Bless us with patience as you lead us along your path, one step at a time. Amen.

Discussion

1. Are you a patient or an impatient person? How has this trait impacted your life?

2. Why do people often find it hard to wait patiently?

3. Why is it important to wait on the Lord?

4. Does waiting on the Lord mean we do nothing? Please explain.

5. When doors are not opening for us, God may be taking the time to re-shape us or to teach us a new lesson, skill, or talent, just as the potter re-shapes the pot.

6. Make a list of personality traits that might make re-shaping in the potter's hand more difficult or unpleasant.

7. What can you do to become more pliable (like soft clay) in God's hands?

APPENDIX B

Recommended Reading

Careers/Employment/Talents/Passion

Bolles, Richard Nelson. *What Color Is Your Parachute? 2007.* Berkeley, CA: Ten Speed Press, 2007 by Richard Nelson Bolles.

Keirsey, David and Marilyn Bates. *Please Understand Me: Character & Temperament Types*, 5th Ed. Del Mar, CA: Prometheus Nemesis Book Company, 1984 by Gnosology Books Ltd.

Rawles, David. *Finding a Job God's Way: Moving into the HOV Lane of Your Career.* Garland, TX: Hannibal Books, 2005 by David Rawles.

God's Will, God's Call

Burtness, Eric. *A Life Worth Leading.* Minneapolis, MN: Augsburg Fortress, 2006 Augsburg Fortress.

Friesen, Garry with J. Robin Maxson. *Decision Making and the Will of God.* Sisters, OR: Multnomah Publishers, 2004 by Garry Friesen.

Smith, Gordon T. *Courage and Calling: Embracing Your God-Given Potential.* Downers Grove, IL: IVP Books, and imprint of InterVarsity Press, 1999 by Gordon T. Smith.

Warren, Rick. *The Purpose Driven Life: What on Earth Am I Here For?* Grand Rapids, MI: Zondervan, 2002 by Rick Warren.

Inspirational/Multiple Topics

Gillmor, Verla. *Reality Check: A Survival Manual for Christians in the Workplace.* Camp Hill, PA: Horizon Books, 2001 by Horizon Books.

God's Priorities for Your Life for Women. Peabody, MA: Hendrickson Publishers, Inc., 2006 Hendrickson Publishers, Inc.

Goodman, Karon Phillips. *You're Late Again, Lord! The Impatient Woman's Guide to God's Timing.* Uhrichsville, OH: Barbour Publishing, 2002 by Karon Phillips Goodman.

Mission/Vision

Bolles, Richard Nelson. *How to Find Your Mission in Life.* Berkeley, CA: Ten Speed Press, 2005 by Richard Nelson Bolles.

Brennfleck, Kevin and Kay Marie Brennfleck. *Live Your Calling: A Practical Guide to Finding and Fulfilling Your Mission in Life.* San Francisco, CA: Josey-Bass, a Wiley Imprint, 2005 by Kevin and Kay Marie Brennfleck.

Transition/Recovery/Healing

Beattie, Melody. *Codependent No More: How to Stop Controlling Others and Start Caring for Yourself.* Center City, MN: Hazelden Foundation, 1992 by Hazelden Foundation.

Bridges, William. *Managing Transitions: Making the Most of Change, 2nd Ed.* Cambridge, MA: Da Capo Press, a member of the Perseus Books Group, 2003 by William Bridges.

Bridges, William. *The Way of Transition: Embracing Life's Most Difficult Moments.* Cambridge, MA: Da Capo Press, a member of the Perseus Books Group, 2001 by William Bridges.

Bridges, William. *Transitions: Making Sense of Life's Changes, 2nd Ed.* Cambridge, MA: Da Capo Press, a member of the Perseus Books Group, 2004 by William Bridges.

Kennedy, D. James. *Turn It to Gold.* Ann Arbor, MI: Servant Publications, 1991 by D. James Kennedy.

Memory Verses

I encourage you to cut out these verses as you work through each chapter, and place them in conspicuous places in your home as a reminder.

Chapter 1: Go Boldly!

Trust in the Lord with all your heart and lean not on your own understanding; in all your ways submit to him, and he will make your paths straight. *Proverbs 3:5–6*	*Trust in the Lord with all your heart and lean not on your own understanding; in all your ways submit to him, and he will make your paths straight.* *Proverbs 3:5–6*
Trust in the Lord with all your heart and lean not on your own understanding; in all your ways submit to him, and he will make your paths straight. *Proverbs 3:5–6*	*Trust in the Lord with all your heart and lean not on your own understanding; in all your ways submit to him, and he will make your paths straight.* *Proverbs 3:5–6*
Trust in the Lord with all your heart and lean not on your own understanding; in all your ways submit to him, and he will make your paths straight. *Proverbs 3:5–6*	*Trust in the Lord with all your heart and lean not on your own understanding; in all your ways submit to him, and he will make your paths straight.* *Proverbs 3:5–6*

Chapter 2: Why Me? Why Now?

Refrain from anger and turn from wrath; do not fret—it leads only to evil. For those who are evil will be destroyed, but those who hope in the Lord will inherit the land. Psalm 37:8–9	Refrain from anger and turn from wrath; do not fret—it leads only to evil. For those who are evil will be destroyed, but those who hope in the Lord will inherit the land. Psalm 37:8–9
Refrain from anger and turn from wrath; do not fret—it leads only to evil. For those who are evil will be destroyed, but those who hope in the Lord will inherit the land. Psalm 37:8–9	Refrain from anger and turn from wrath; do not fret—it leads only to evil. For those who are evil will be destroyed, but those who hope in the Lord will inherit the land. Psalm 37:8–9

Chapter 3: Worry, Worry, Worry

Cast all your anxiety on him because he cares for you. 1 Peter 5:7	Cast all your anxiety on him because he cares for you. 1 Peter 5:7
Cast all your anxiety on him because he cares for you. 1 Peter 5:7	Cast all your anxiety on him because he cares for you. 1 Peter 5:7

Chapter 4: Rejected Again

Blessed is the one who perseveres under trial, because having stood the test, that person will receive the crown of life that the Lord has promised to those who love him. *James 1:12*	*Blessed is the one who perseveres under trial, because having stood the test, that person will receive the crown of life that the Lord has promised to those who love him.* *James 1:12*
Blessed is the one who perseveres under trial, because having stood the test, that person will receive the crown of life that the Lord has promised to those who love him. *James 1:12*	*Blessed is the one who perseveres under trial, because having stood the test, that person will receive the crown of life that the Lord has promised to those who love him.* *James 1:12*

Chapter 5: Your Destination

Since, then, you have been raised with Christ, set your hearts on things above, where Christ is seated at the right hand of God. Set your minds on things above, not on earthly things. *Colossians 3:1–2*	*Since, then, you have been raised with Christ, set your hearts on things above, where Christ is seated at the right hand of God. Set your minds on things above, not on earthly things.* *Colossians 3:1–2*
Since, then, you have been raised with Christ, set your hearts on things above, where Christ is seated at the right hand of God. Set your minds on things above, not on earthly things. *Colossians 3:1–2*	*Since, then, you have been raised with Christ, set your hearts on things above, where Christ is seated at the right hand of God. Set your minds on things above, not on earthly things.* *Colossians 3:1–2*

Chapter 6: God Called

Come to me with your ears wide open. *Listen, and you will find life.* *Isaiah 55:3 NLT*	*Come to me with your ears wide open.* *Listen, and you will find life.* *Isaiah 55:3 NLT*
Come to me with your ears wide open. *Listen, and you will find life.* *Isaiah 55:3 NLT*	*Come to me with your ears wide open.* *Listen, and you will find life.* *Isaiah 55:3 NLT*

Chapter 7: When In Doubt, Start With His Command

And whatever you do, whether in word or deed, do it all in the name of the Lord Jesus, giving thanks to God the Father through him. *Colossians 3:17*	*And whatever you do, whether in word or deed, do it all in the name of the Lord Jesus, giving thanks to God the Father through him.* *Colossians 3:17*
And whatever you do, whether in word or deed, do it all in the name of the Lord Jesus, giving thanks to God the Father through him. *Colossians 3:17*	*And whatever you do, whether in word or deed, do it all in the name of the Lord Jesus, giving thanks to God the Father through him.* *Colossians 3:17*

Chapter 8: Here I Am; I'll Do It!

Teach me to do your will, for you are my God; may your good Spirit lead me on level ground. *Psalm 143:10*	*Teach me to do your will, for you are my God; may your good Spirit lead me on level ground.* *Psalm 143:10*
Teach me to do your will, for you are my God; may your good Spirit lead me on level ground. *Psalm 143:10*	*Teach me to do your will, for you are my God; may your good Spirit lead me on level ground.* *Psalm 143:10*

Chapter 9: Action, Action, Action

Each of you should use whatever gift you have received to serve others, as faithful stewards of God's grace in its various forms. *1 Peter 4:10*	*Each of you should use whatever gift you have received to serve others, as faithful stewards of God's grace in its various forms.* *1 Peter 4:10*
Each of you should use whatever gift you have received to serve others, as faithful stewards of God's grace in its various forms. *1 Peter 4:10*	*Each of you should use whatever gift you have received to serve others, as faithful stewards of God's grace in its various forms.* *1 Peter 4:10*

Chapter 10: Growth Opportunities

And we know that in all things God works for the good of those who love him, who have been called according to his purpose. *Romans 8:28*	*And we know that in all things God works for the good of those who love him, who have been called according to his purpose.* *Romans 8:28*
And we know that in all things God works for the good of those who love him, who have been called according to his purpose. *Romans 8:28*	*And we know that in all things God works for the good of those who love him, who have been called according to his purpose.* *Romans 8:28*

Chapter 11: One Step at a Time

There is a time for everything, and a season for every activity under the heavens. *Ecclesiastes 3:1*	*There is a time for everything, and a season for every activity under the heavens.* *Ecclesiastes 3:1*
There is a time for everything, and a season for every activity under the heavens. *Ecclesiastes 3:1*	*There is a time for everything, and a season for every activity under the heavens.* *Ecclesiastes 3:1*

About the Author

She's an amphitheater wannabe. That is who Sheila M. Luck is. She heard God calling in 2001. After arguing with God about this call for two and a half years, Sheila finally responded to God with a resounding, "Well, okay, if you insist." Although reluctant then, she knows it was the best move she ever made. Now Sheila wants to be an amphitheater for God's kingdom, sharing God's love with anyone who will listen to her presentations or read her books.

It has been an unusual path, getting to this place in life. Being an amphitheater for God's kingdom was not Sheila's plan. It wasn't on her radar screen. Still, after publishing three Bible studies and now this book (with more to come), she occasionally wonders why God chose her. She realizes that the answer doesn't matter. What matters? She said yes.

Following college, Sheila began her career working as an engineer for IBM. After three years, she resigned to attend law school at Marquette University Law School, graduating in 1985. Following graduation from law school, she and her husband Wayne moved to Texas, where she was employed as an attorney for Exxon Production

Research Company, Exxon Company USA, and Exxon Company International. After nearly ten years, for family reasons, Sheila, Wayne, and their two young daughters moved to Wisconsin, where she worked as in-house legal counsel for a utility company and later for a paper company. At her last employer, Sheila worked in a dual capacity as senior legal counsel and human resources director.

She retired from this line of work in 2003, when she accepted God's call to begin writing Christian books and speaking for a variety of Christian organizations. Sheila's current books include the following:

My Baby's Feet: Choice, Death and the Aftermath

The Challenge of Change: Careers, Callings and Work-Life Crossroads

My Secret Loss: Finding Life After Abortion

Grapple with Guilt, Shed the Shame

Additional books are coming soon. Keep an eye on her website or her author page on Facebook to hear the latest news.

It is Sheila's personal and company mission to promote positive change by helping others make quality choices for themselves personally and in their work-lives. Consistent with this mission, in 2008, Sheila began offering mediation services. Mediation enables people to resolve their conflicts in a mutually agreeable manner. The goal is to help the parties reach a solution that they can live with in a timely and economical manner.

Although her business is not currently a non-profit or not-for-profit organization, Sheila returns all income into her efforts as an amphitheater for God's kingdom.

Sheila serves on the board of directors of Elizabeth Ministry International, Inc. and Wisconsin Right to Life. She is also a monthly columnist for *Wisconsin Christian News.*

Sheila received a bachelor of science degree in industrial technology from the University of Wisconsin-Platteville in 1979, a juris doctor degree from Marquette University Law School in 1985, and a Certificate of Completion in Equipping from The Masters Institute in 2011.

For more about Sheila Luck, her books, and speaking engagements, please check out her website: www.connectingchoices.com. You are also invited to "Like" her author page on Facebook: www.facebook.com/sheilamluck, where you will find information on her Facebook chat groups and on her blog, as these items are developed. She is also on LinkedIn, ShoutLife.com, and Plaxo.

If this book helped you, review it on Amazon: The Upside to Job Loss

Available where books are sold

In the Jubilee Bible, the usage and context tends to define each key word so you don't need to depend on theological dictionaries or reference materials. Careful attention has been made to properly translate the first usage of each key word and through to the last occurrence. Then, as the word makes its way across the Old Testament and you make the correct match with the corresponding Greek word in the New Testament, an amazing pattern emerges. The Jubilee Bible is the only translation we know of that has each unique Hebrew word matched and mated with a unique English word so that the usage (number of occurrences and number of verses where the word occurs) sets forth a meaningful number pattern and a complete definition of what God means by each word.

www.ingramcontent.com/pod-product-compliance
Lightning Source LLC
LaVergne TN
LVHW051549070426
835507LV00021B/2492